Lights Out at Midnight

Lights Out at Midnight

Evangelist Beverly Yokley
Laura Newberry-Yokley

© 2018

Lights Out at Midnight
Written by Evangelist Beverly Yokley and
Laura Newberry-Yokley

Copyright © 2018
Sonrisa Products

All rights reserved. This book or any portion thereof
may not be reproduced or used in any manner
whatsoever without the express written permission of
the publisher except for the use of brief quotations in a
book review or scholarly journal.

First Printing: 2018

ISBN-13: 978-0692154588
ISBN-10: 0692154582

Sonrisa Products
1527 Willoughby Drive
Wooster, OH 44691
sonrisaproducts.com
001-614-202-2198

Printed in the United States of America

*"I am crucified with Christ:
nevertheless I live;
not I, but Christ liveth in me:
and the life which I now live in the flesh
I live by the faith of the Son of God,
who loved me, and gave himself for me."
Galatians 2:20*

To my husband Charles
and The Yokley Family.

Table of Contents

Introduction	9
Part I: Lights Out at Midnight	**15**
Waiting in Vigilance	16
Kingdom	18
Lights Out at Midnight	20
Virgin	23
Lamp	27
Bridesgroom	31
Foolish Virgins	36
Wedding Dress	40
Rebel with a Cause	45
Holiness or Hell?	49
Watch	56
Part II: Romance & Relationship	**61**
Charge it to My Account	62
Ain't Got No Problem	65
Ain't Got No Problem – Charge It	68
Sexy Feet	71
The Love of God	77
1. Communication	79
2. Marriage	89
3. Discipline	96
4. Love	108
Part III: Any Word from God?	**115**
Is There Any Word from the Lord	116
What is God Saying to You?	122
God Knows My Name	125
God Changes Not!	129

Part IV: Jesus & Me	**135**
For unto Us a Child Is Born	136
Can Anything Good Come Out of Nazareth?	143
Must Jesus Bear the Cross?	152
When I See Jesus—Amen!	158
What is Jesus Doing for Me?	162
Part V: Jesus & You	**169**
What Do You Want Jesus to Do?	170
It's All About Jesus. It's Not About You!	175
Has Jesus Chosen You to Be His Friend?	178
Whatever You Do, Be Like Jesus	185
Small Words of Jesus	189
Appendix	*195*

Introduction

I have been preaching for over 40 years in the Original Church of God. This book is a collection of sermons and study guides that I have written over the years.

My daughter-in-law, Laura Newberry-Yokley, has written down my sermons here, dividing them into five themes: Lights Out at Midnight, Romance & Relationship, Any Word from God?, Jesus & Me, and Jesus & You. We have connected in a special way through the writing of this book.

Laura will tell you that she has gotten to know and understands my Love for God in an intimate and personal way. To share in the writing down of my sermons, she has entered into the biggest bible study of her lifetime. She has told me many times that in the process of writing this book, she has deepened her own Love for God. I suspect that our readers will do the same.

Laura and I would meet on the phone every Saturday to go over each outline together. For two years, I would recreate each sermon over the phone to her, as she crafted the sermons from my original outlines. Preaching on the phone, the sermons would come to life; they take on a life of their own, once embodied, once spoken.

Writing this book has been a powerful experience for both of us. In 2010, I got very sick. God said to me, "Lights Out at Midnight." If I'm ready to go, I told God, "I've got oil in my lamp and I'm ready to come see you. If not, I'm prepared to meet you." But God had other plans!

The idea for *Lights Out at Midnight* came to me when I was very ill. At that time, my daughter-in-law, Laura, stuck the following note in my Bible when I was in the hospital in 2010, her healing prayer based on Psalm 91, my favorite Psalm.

> For Mrs. Yokley,
> Abide in the shadow of the Almighty. He is your refuge and your fortress. In Him you can trust. You shall be covered with His feathers and under His wings. Trust Him. He is your shield. Pestilence cannot reach you. It shall not come near you. The Lord is your habitation. No evil shall befall you. His angels are all over thee and will keep you always. His love is set upon you. He knows your name. Love you!
> -Laura

Three years later, Laura also got very sick. She stopped breathing for thirty seconds and had a near death experience. In that time, she recalls going to see God, but He told her that she had a lot of work to do, so He sent her back. She realized after this experience that this life that we've created here, including our personalities, what we do for a living, and how we dress up to go out, is a posture and does not have anything to do with our relationship with God. We also can't take any of it with us. God is calling each of us to speak up and out about God!

When I first sent Laura my sermon notes to begin writing them down, I sent her a copy of her original note from 2010, and on the back, I wrote:

Laura,

Do you remember this? I keep it in my Bible. Remember that these words cover Laura, too!

Love,

Mom/GG

Psalm 91   *The State of the Godly*

1   He that dwelleth in the secret place of the most High shall abide under the shadow of the Almighty.

2   I will say of the Lord, He is my refuge and my fortress: my God; in him will I trust.

3   Surely he shall deliver thee from the snare of the fowler, and from the noisome pestilence.

4   He shall cover thee with his feathers, and under his wings shalt thou trust: his truth shall be thy shield and buckler.

5   Thou shalt not be afraid for the terror by night; nor for the arrow that flieth by day;

6   Nor for the pestilence that walketh in darkness; nor for the destruction that wasteth at noonday.

7   A thousand shall fall at thy side, and then thousand at thy right hand; but it shall not come nigh thee.

8   Only with thine eyes shalt thou behold and see the reward of the wicked.

9   Because thou hast made the Lord, which is my refuge, even the most High, thy habitation;

10   There shall be no evil befall thee, neither shall any plague come nigh thy dwelling.

11   For he shall give his angels charge over thee, to keep thee in all thy ways.

12   They shall bear thee up in their hands, lest thou dash thy foot against a stone.

13   Thou shalt tread upon the lion and adder: the young lion and the dragon shalt thou trample under feet.

14   Because he hath set his love upon me, therefore will I deliver him: I will set him on high, because he hath known my name.
15   He shall call upon me, and I will answer him: I will be with him in trouble; I will deliver him, and honour him.
16   With long life will I satisfy him, and show him my salvation

May these words comfort our readers!

We never know when our "Lights Out at Midnight" moment will come. But when it does, we must be ready. Both of us have been given a second chance. Life is full of second chances for all of us. What a blessing for us to love each other through working with the Word of God!

As we began writing our book together, we acknowledged that there was a certain apprehension that bubbled up. Putting yourself out there is scary, and finally pushing print is equally as difficult. **We discovered that fear is real.** Or false evidence appearing real.

Fear, in our modern world, is defined as "an unpleasant emotion caused by the belief that someone or something is dangerous, likely to cause pain, or a threat." It can often affect our voice, stall our actions, and make us feel inadequate.

But fear in the Bible also means something else. Fear is a feeling of reverence, awe, and respect. It can be directed toward God or another human being. It can be either healthful or harmful. It is our choice how we wish to express fear.

Acts 2:43

43   And fear came upon every soul; and many wonders and signs were done by the apostles.

The good news is that fear can be overcome. As we wrote these pages, we remembered the healthful and reverent side of fear, giving Glory to God every step of the way. We withdrew care for the outcome and appreciated the process of living with God's Word, working in prayer, and loving each other.

The sermons are written here as sermon guides for you to use in your own preaching, Bible study, and personal practice. This particular series is comprised of sermons beginning in 2010 through 2015. They continue through time, touching upon different themes, symbols, metaphors, and topics from the Bible. They are arranged chronologically and according to theme. At the end, you will find a reference of all the Bible verses that I have discussed in my sermons in order as they occur in the Bible. We have used the King James Version of the Bible.

It is my hope that you are inspired by these sermons, too, in the way that they are recorded here. Laura has learned in the writing down of my sermons to explore God's Word and listen to what He is speaking through her life. I hope that you will you listen to what God speaks through your life by reading this book, but also may the Word of God live in your everyday life. Inside the spoken Word of preaching exists God's Word coming through us. While God's Word is here on paper, we encourage you to make these sermons your own, embodying them in your own way.

Preach them with your own interpretation of how you experience God. Study these pages; take what you need and leave the rest. And may the Lord be always with you!

Part I:
Lights Out at Midnight Sermons from 2010-2012

Waiting in Vigilance

The Kingdom, or death, might come when you least expect it. That's why it is important to always be ready, to wait in vigilance.

The Kingdom of God or the Kingdom of Heaven is an experience of blessedness, very much like the Garden of Eden. In both, evil has been overcome, where one only knows of great happiness and everlasting peace. It is also a place you go after you pass on from this lifetime.

Matthew 25 tells of a story about the Wise and Foolish Maidens, which tells of a delay. It is understood that death has already overtaken them. They are waiting for Jesus to return.

The story mentions virgins, lamps, and a bridegroom. Each can be interpreted symbolically, which will be discussed in further detail.

Sermon Outline

    10 virgins
    10 lamps
    1 bridegroom

Matthew 25:1-13
1   Then shall the kingdom of heaven be likened unto ten virgins, which took their lamps, and went forth to meet the bridegroom.
2   And five of them were wise, and five were foolish.
3   They that were foolish took their lamps, and took no oil with them:
4   but the wise took oil in their vessels with their lamps.
5   While the bridegroom tarried, they all slumbered and slept.
6   And at midnight there was a cry made, Behold, the bridegroom cometh; go ye out to meet him.
7   Then all those virgins arose, and trimmed their lamps.
8   And the foolish said unto the wise, Give us of your oil; for our lamps are gone out.
9   but the wise answered, saying, Not so; lest there be not enough for us and you: but go ye rather to them that sell, and buy for yourselves.
10   And while they went to buy, the bridegroom came; and they that were ready went in with him to the marriage: and the door was shut.
11   Afterward came also the other virgins, saying, Lord, Lord, open to us.
12   But he answered and said, Verily I say unto you, I know you not.
13   Watch therefore, for ye know neither the day nor the hour wherein the Son of man cometh.

Kingdom

Jesus often taught in story or used parable to make a point. The Greek meaning of parable is "to throw alongside of." And Jesus was often considered, and even referred to in Scripture, as a teacher.

In the story of the sower, found in Matthew 13, Jesus tells of a sower, who went out to sprinkle his seeds. These seeds would grow into crops, and during harvest time, they would be gathered and harvested.

In the story of the sower, the seed is like man, who is good. Yet, Jesus says that some of the seeds did not go into places that were well suited for plants to grow. They fell among the stones and thrones, while others did manage to fall on good ground.

No matter where you are planted, though, you must work to get into the Kingdom of Heaven.

Sermon Outline

God created the heaven and earth – the good man, right seed.

Matthew 13:24
24 Another parable put he forth unto them, saying, The kingdom of heaven is likened unto a man which sowed good seed in his field.

He made man in His image.

Matthew 13:26
26 But when the blade was sprung up, and brought forth fruit, then appeared the tares also.

That old serpent, the devil.

Matthew 13:25
25 But while men slept, his enemy came and sowed tares among the wheat, and went his way.

Until harvest time—
Lights Out at Midnight.

Matthew 13:30
30 Let both grow together until the harvest: and in the time of harvest I will say to the reapers, Gather ye together first the tares, and bind them in bundles to burn them: but gather the wheat into my barn.

Lights Out at Midnight

The story continues that a man went out to hire workers to harvest his vineyard. He went out early in the morning, then again at the third, sixth, ninth, and eleventh hours. In each case, he agreed to pay the workers for their work but was not willing to pay workers as they stood idle.

Working to get into the Kingdom must be a continuous process that you work at all day, every day. God will reward you for your hard work, but he will not reward you to stand by.

What will you be doing at your "harvest time"? Will you be working to get into the Kingdom of Heaven, or will you be standing idle?

Sermon Outline

Early.

Matthew 20:1
1   *For the kingdom of heaven is like unto a man that is an householder, which went out early in the morning to hire labourers into his vineyard.*

Third hour.

Matthew 20:3
3   *And he went out about the third hour, and saw others standing idle in the marketplace,*

Sixth and ninth hours.

Matthew 20:5
5   *Again he went out about the sixth and ninth hour, and did likewise.*

Eleventh hour.

Matthew 20:6
6   *And about the eleventh hour he went out, and found others standing idle, and saith unto them, Why stand ye here all the day idle?*

WORK—get in the Kingdom. **Lights Out at Midnight**. Just remember, but a few.

Matthew 20:16
16   So the last shall be first, and the first last: for many be called, but few chosen.

Virgin

A virgin is committed to God and loves Him. A virgin wants to get married and get into Heaven. He or she is willing to give it all up for God and is in a constant state of preparing.

Life is like a journey. All ten virgins started out on this journey but not all of them were prepared.

Matthew 25:1
1   *...And went forth to meet the bridegroom.*

A virgin can be compared with the earth in the parable of the sower. The seeds may spring up in stony places but their roots, or depth, were not able to sustain them.

Matthew 13:3
3   *And he spake many things until them in parables, saying, Behold, a sower went forth to sow;*

Sermon Outline

A virgin is defined as:
- Committed
- Loves God
- Wants to get into Heaven
- Willing to give it all up
- Prepared

Went forth to meet. Life is like a journey. All ten virgins started out on this journey but not all of them were prepared.
Parable of the sower/seed they spring up – have no depth.

Matthew 3:3-9
5   Some fell upon stony places, where they had not much earth: and forthwith they sprung up, because they had no deepness of earth:

Wayside seeds can be compared with Sunday morning Christians, people who have made no commitment to the Lord. The seed doesn't take hold, devoured quickly, and forgotten. Christ doesn't take hold because it's not part of their life.

Matthew 13:4
4   And when he sowed, some seeds fell by the way side, and the fowls came and devoured them up:

Seeds that fall in stony places sprung up, but have no depth. Sunday morning Christians have a lamp but no oil. They have emotional ties to going to church, they come to church every Sunday. They hear the Word but they don't perceive what is going on.

Matthew 13:5-6
5   Some fell upon stony places, where they had not much earth: and forthwith they sprung up, because they had no deepness of earth:
6   And when the sun was up, they were scorched; and because they had no root, they withered away.

Seeds that fall on thorny places can be compared with the foolish virgins. Because of worldly cares, they can come to church, get to the Bible study when they can, but they need work. They say that the Lord knows their hearts. They are the financial givers – their lamp is full of oil.

Matthew 13:7
7   And some fell among thorns; and the thorns sprung up, and choked them:

The seeds that fall on good ground are the Christians who have accepted Jesus Christ as their Savior. They have their lamp and their oil in the lamp and are okay. They get extra oil too. They are always ready. They have prepared their whole life. Midnight is a joyful time. They can't wait for the bridegroom to return.

Matthew 13:8
8   But other fell into good ground, and brought for fruit, some an hundredfold, some sixtyfold, some thirtyfold.

Lamp

Our lives are like journeys. We are walking along a path that is dark. God is our lamp that lights our way. Light is illuminating and can also be interpreted as a symbol of God's presence. A lamp will guide our way through the thrones and the stony places.

A lamp will only work if you have oil to light it. On Sunday mornings, there are a lot of people in the church pews who have a lamp but no oil. Perhaps their lack of oil comes in the form of an emotional or some other kind of barrier. Perhaps their barrier is financial. Whatever their barrier, or lack of oil, God can light the way. God is the giver of the lamp *and* the oil.

Sermon Outline

1. The Lord is the lamp and the oil.

2 Samuel 22:1-29 (David's Thanksgiving)
1   *And David spake unto the Lord the words of this song in the day that the Lord had delivered him out of the hand of all his enemies, and out of the hand of Saul;*
2   *And he said, The Lord is my rock, and my fortress, and my deliverer;*
3   *The God of my rock; in him will I trust: he is my shield, and the horn of my salvation, my high tower, and my refuge, my saviour; thou savest me from violence.*
4   *I will call on the Lord, who is worthy to be praised: so shall I be saved from mine enemies.*
5   *When the waves of death compassed me, the floods of ungodly men made me afraid;*
6   *The sorrows of hell compassed me about; the snares of death prevented me;*
7   *In my distress I called upon the Lord, and cried to my God: and he did hear my voice out of his temple, and my cry did enter into his ears.*
8   *Then the earth shook and trembled; the foundations of heaven moved and shook, because he was wroth.*
9   *There went up a smoke out of his nostrils, and fire out of his mouth devoured: coals were kindled by it.*
10   *He bowed the heavens also, and came down; and darkness was under his feet.*
11   *And he rode upon a cherub, and did fly: and he was seen upon the wings of the wind.*
12   *He was made darkness pavilions round about him, dark waters, and thick clouds of the skies.*

13   Through the brightness before him were coals of fire kindled.
14   The Lord thundered from heaven, and the most High uttered his voice.
15   And he sent out arrows, and scattered them; lightning, and discomfited them.
16   And the channels of the sea appeared, the foundations of the world were discovered, at the rebuking of the Lord, at the blast of the breath of his nostrils.
17   He sent from above, he took me; he drew me out of many waters;
18   He delivered me from my strong enemy, and from them that hated me: for they were too strong for me.
19   They prevented me in the day of my calamity: but the Lord was my stay.
20   He brought me forth also into a large place: he delivered me, because he delighted in me.
21   The Lord rewarded me according to my righteousness: according to the cleanness of my hands hath he recompensed me.
22   For I have kept the ways of the Lord, and have not wickedly departed from my God.
23   For all his judgments were before me: and as for his statutes, I did not depart from them.
24   I was also upright before him, and have kept myself from mine iniquity.
25   Therefore the Lord hath recompensed me according to my righteousness; according to my cleanness in his eye sight.
26   With the merciful thou wilt show thyself merciful, and with the upright man thou wilt show thyself upright.
27   With the pure thou wilt show thyself pure; and with the forward thou wilt show thyself unsavoury.
28   And the afflicted people thou wilt save: but thine eyes are upon the haughty, that thou mayest bring them down.

29   For thou art my lamp, O Lord: and the Lord will lighten m darkness.

2. All received a lamp and set up for his liking.

2 Samuel 15:4
4   Absalom said moreover, Oh that I were made judge in the land, that every man which hath any suit or cause might come unto me, and I would do him justice!

3. Word is a lamp unto my feet and a light.

Psalm 119:105
105   Thy word is a lamp unto my feed, and a light unto my path.

Bridesgroom

A bridesgroom is a man who has just married, or is about to be married. The Bridesgroom is often associated with Jesus. John the Baptist called Jesus "the Bridegroom."

John 3:29
He that hath the bride is the bridegroom: but the friend of the bridegroom, which standeth and heareth him, rejoiceth greatly because of the bridegroom's voice: this my joy therefore is filled.

Jesus also referred to himself as a bridegroom.

Matthew 9:15
15   And Jesus said unto them, Can the children of the bridechamber mourn, as long as the bridegroom is with them? But the days will come, when the bridegroom shall be taken from them, and then shall they fast.

If Jesus is referred to as a bridesgroom, then who is His bride? Is His bride the church? Or those who are followers of Him? Those married to him by their faith?

Sermon Outline

The beloved Son of God is God's *only* son.

John 3:16
16   For God so loved the world, that he gave his only begotten Son, that whosoever believeth in him should not perish, but have everlasting life.

God's Son's job was to be a savior.

John 3:17
17   For God sent not his Son into the world to condemn the world; but that the world through him might be saved.

He started young.

Luke 2:41-49
49   And he said unto them, How is that ye sought me? wist ye not that I must be about my Father's business?

Oneness with God.

John 10:30
30   I and my Father are one.

Matthew 3:17
17   And lo a voice from heaven, saying, This is my beloved Son, in whom I am well pleased.

The pre-existence of Jesus.

John 1:1-14; 8:58

1   In the beginning was the Word, and the Word was with God, and the Word was God.

2   The same was in the beginning with God.

3   All things were made by him; and without him was not any thing made that was made.

4   In him was life; and the life was the light of men.

5   And the light shineth in darkness; and the darkness comprehended it not.

6   There was a man sent from God, whose name was John.

7   The same came for a witness, to bear witness of the Light, that all men through him might believe.

8   He was in the world, and the world was made by him, and the world knew him not.

9   That was the true Light, which lighteth every man that cometh into the world.

10   He was in the world, and the world was made by him, and the world knew him not.

11   He came unto his own, and his own received him not.

12   But as many as received him, to them gave he power to become the sons of God, even to them that believed on his name:

13   Which were born, not of blood, nor of the will of the flesh, nor of the will of man, but of God.

14   And the Word was made flesh, and dwelt among us, (and we beheld his glory, the glory as of the only begotten of the Father,) full of grace and truth.

John 8:58

58   Jesus said unto them, Verily, verily, I say unto you, Before Abraham was, I am.

Jesus, the bridegroom, has authority; all power.

Matthew 28:18
18   And Jesus came and spake unto them, saying, All power is given unto me in heaven and in earth.

Jesus, the Bridegroom, has power and authority over:

Nature.

Matthew 8:27
27   But the men marveled, saying, What manner of man is this, that even the winds and the sea obey him!

Matthew 11:27
27   All things are delivered unto me of my Father: and no man knoweth the Son, but the Father; neither knoweth any man the Father, save the Son, and he to whomsoever the Son will reveal him.

John 3:35
35   The Father loveth the Son, and hath given all things into his hand.

Heaven.

I Peter 3:22
22   Who is gone into heaven, and is on the right hand of God; angels and authorities and powers being made subject unto him.

The church.

Ephesians 1:22
22   And hath put all things under his feet, and gave him to be the head over all things to the church,

Holiness.

I Peter 1:15-16
15   But as he which hath called you is holy, so be ye holy in all manner of conversation;
16   Because it is written, Be ye holy; for I am holy.

Strong man to run a race.

Psalms 19:5
5   Which is as a bridegroom coming out of his chamber, and rejoiceth as a strong man to run a race.

Foolish Virgins

The Bible tells us to examine ourselves.

It isn't our job to figure out what everybody else is doing, whether they are saved or not. And our job isn't to save everyone else, either. It is our job to make sure we have enough oil for our own salvation.

Lights Out at Midnight. We can assure ourselves that the lights are going out for all of us. Each of us knows where we stand with God.

In the story of the five wise virgins and five foolish, each of us is waiting for the Bridegroom to come. Some of us have enough oil, but some of us do not.

Sermon Outline

Yes, **Lights Out at Midnight**, but for the five wise virgins, the light and life had just begun. Why? Because they had oil in their lamps when the cry came out. Did the other five virgins also have oil? Yes, but they did not have extra oil to last until the door was open. Let's look at these five virgins, who did not have extra oil. They were virgins, which means that they had accept Jesus as their Savior. They had oil at the beginning of the night, to begin their wait for the midnight hour.

The First Virgin of the Foolish:
They want God to do all the work. They want Him to take everything from them when He wants to. They are not willing to give up anything on their own. They have just enough spirit for Sunday morning. God is everything, but "their shoes," meaning their daily walk with God, is not there.

The Second Virgin of the Foolish:
They are "O' you worthy." They just want to praise God. These are the "First giving honor to God" virgins. Whenever they have an opportunity, they give a shout out, but their life is not worthy of extra oil.

The Third Virgin of the Foolish:
This is the group of virgins who see only the super-powerful side of God, their supernatural, all powerful God. They look for the out pouring of the spirit, "The Big Bang," supernatural experience that is only an outward showing.

The Fourth Virgin of the Foolish:

This is a group of crying saints. Luke 11:34 says, "The light of the body is the eyes...but when thine eye is evil; thy body also is full of darkness."

Luke 11:34
34 The light of the body is the eye: therefore when thine eye is single, thy whole body also is full of light; but when thine eye is evil, thy body also is full of darkness.

This group believes that it does not take all that to go to Heaven. They make up their own standards for Salvation. They may drink a little, go clubbing a little, swear a little, and change the standards of the church a little. They just cry on songs and sleep on The Word. When the music is going, they're singing and shouting, but when it comes time to understand the Word, they are either asleep mentally or physically.

The Fifth Virgin of the Foolish:

This group of virgins are left at home. We all love the story about the prodigal son, but some Christians are the son that was left at home, the oldest son, who does everything right and is still lost in his own house. This group has access to everything, even raised in Holiness, but they don't realize that they have their Father's Love all along. They may not recognize God's blessings.

Luke 15:25-30
25   Now his elder son was in the field: and as he came and drew nigh to the house, he heard music and dancing.

26   And he called one of the servants, and asked what these things meant.
27   And he said unto him, Thy brother is come; and thy father hath killed the fatted calf, because he hath received him safe and sound.
28   And he was angry, and would not go in: therefore came his father out, and entreated him.
29   And he answering said to his father, Lo, these many years do I serve thee, neither transgressed I at any time thy commandment: and yet thou never gavest me a kid, that I might make merry with my friends:
30   But as soon as this thy son was come, which hath devoured thy living with harlots, thou hast killed for him the fatted calf.

All that God has is theirs, but they did not make use of God's blessings and power.

Luke 15:31
31   And he said unto him, Son, thou art ever with me, and all that I have is thine.

Wedding Dress

Many of us have probably forgotten why we wear a white wedding dress when we get married. White is symbolic of purity and virginity. Long past are the days that most of us wait until marriage to have sex with someone. Wearing white used to mean that your virginity was still intact – and that was also associated with purity.

A wedding is a marriage ceremony. Among the Israelites, the whole community participated.

The dress is symbolic of your armor. God's armor against sin. Against the wickedness of the world and of the devil's wiles.

Sermon Outline

Go Ye Out to Meet Him. Check yourself out. Self-examination. Do you love the Lord?

Song: "Is there anybody here who loves my Jesus? Is there anybody here who loves the Lord? I want to know if you love the Lord."

I am committed. I give myself away so you can use me. Is my lamp burning brightly? Do I have enough oil in my lamp? "Give me oil in my lamp, keep it burning?"

Is my wedding dress really white and without a blemish?

Ephesians 5:25-27
25 *Husbands, love your wives, even as Christ also loved the church, and gave himself for it;*
26 *That he might sanctify and cleanse it with the washing of water by the word,*
27 *That he might present it to himself a glorious church, not having spot, or wrinkle, or any such thing; but it should be holy and without blemish.*

White: glorious, no spot, no wrinkle. Baby, no blemish.

Ephesians 6:10
10 *Finally, my brethren, be strong in the Lord, and in the power of his might.*

Put on the whole armor of God – The white wedding dress.

Ephesians 6:11
11   Put on the whole armor of God, that ye may be able to stand against the wiles of the devil.

This dress cannot be lost through slumber. I must be able to stand against the wiles of the devil. Remember that it does not matter whether the first laborer goes to work for the Lord or the last.

You must:
1. Love the Lord
2. Must be committed.
3. Have you lamp burning bright, having extra oil.

Because **Lights Out at Midnight**. We must work while it is day.

Ephesians 6: 12-13
12   For we wrestle not against flesh and blood, but against principalities, against powers, against the rulers of the darkness of this world, against spiritual wickedness in high places.
13   Wherefore take unto you the whole armour of God, that ye may be able to withstand in the evil day, and having done all, to stand.

Stand.

Matthew 25:7
7   Then all those virgins arose, and trimmed their lamps.

But not all had on their <u>whole</u> armor of God – the dress was white – glorious, but not holy.

To be holy you must:
- Have your <u>loins girdled</u> with Truth
- <u>Breastplate</u> of Righteousness
- <u>Feet-shod</u> with the preparation of Gospel of Peace
- <u>Shield</u> of Faith
- <u>Helmet</u> of Salvation
- <u>Sword</u> of Spirit (here your extra oil)

Ephesians 6:14-18
14 Stand therefore, having your loins girt about with truth, and having on the breastplate of righteousness;
15 And your feet shod with the preparation of the gospel of peace;
16 Above all, taking the shield of faith, wherewith ye shall be able to quench all the fiery darts of the wicked.
17 And take the helmet of salvation, and the sword of the Spirit, which is the word of God:
18 Praying always with all prayer and supplication in the Spirit, and watching thereunto with all perseverance and supplication for all saints;

Yes, I love the Lord.
Yes, I am committed to Church works.
Yes, I have my lamp and extra oil.
I am a wise bride!

Lights Out at Midnight.
But if you don't have any oil? You need the Word of God to direct/lead you through the wiles of the devil.

Ephesians 6:12
12   For we wrestle not against flesh and blood, but against principalities, against powers, against the rulers of the darkness of this world, against spiritual wickedness in high places.

As a bride, you must have extra oil because **Lights Out at Midnight**.

Rebel with a Cause

There was a movie called, "A Rebel without a Cause." It was very popular back in the day (1955). James Dean plays Jim Stark, who is the new kid in town. He is rebellious with a troubled past. He must prove himself to the other kids and is willing to do whatever it takes. James Dean's movie was before most of your time. A rebel is a person who goes against the norm.

Jesus was also a rebel, but he was not a rebel without a cause, like Jim Stark. He was a rebel *with* a cause. The church and its ministry can also be today's version of a rebel *with* a cause.

We live in a world of sin. Once we accept Jesus Christ as our Savior, we do not practice sin. We can live in Grace and Holiness instead. We can be washed by the blood of Jesus Christ, who cleanses us of our sins.

The church world of Jesus' time was the Jews. Yes, Jesus was a rebel of his time.

Matthew 13:57
57   And they were offended in him. But Jesus said unto them, A profit is not without honour, save in his own country, and in his own house.

Sermon Outline

Now, Jesus is known in almost every country. Churches are overrun with people.
Lights Out at Midnight.

Matthew 25:1-4
1   Then shall the kingdom of heaven be likened unto ten virgins, which took their lamps, and went forth to meet the bridegroom.
2   And five of them were wise, and five were foolish.
3   They that were foolish took their lamps, and took no oil with them:
4   but the wise took oil in their vessels with their lamps.

This is what the church world looks like today. Five wise and five foolish with an oil problem. Yet all were rebels with a cause.

Yet who is the rebel of today?
- We sin a little. No one is free from sin.
- I am a sinner saved by grace.
- What about the unknown sin?
- David, a man after God's own heart, sinned.
- In a world where the church world doesn't have any oil.

I am a rebel with a cause.

Romans 6:15
15   What then? Shall we sin, because we are not under the law, but under grace? God forbid.

Romans 6:1-4
1   *What shall we say then? Shall we continue in sin, that grace may abound?*
2   *God forbid. How shall we, that are dead to sin, live any longer therein?*
3   *Know ye not, that so many of us as were baptized into Jesus Christ were baptized into his death?*
4   *Therefore we are buried with him by baptism into death: that like as Christ was raised up from the dead by the glory of the Father, even so we also should walk in newness of life.*

Are you that rebel walking upright with oil in your lamp and extra oil for your journey?

James 4:7
7   *Submit yourselves therefore to God. Resist the devil, and he will flee from you.*

Are you resisting the devil, the world, and the church world? Are you living for Christ? Is your walk redeeming the time?

Colossians 4:5
5   *Walk in wisdom toward them that are without, redeeming the time.*

Are you choosing to be a rebel?

Hebrews 11:25
25   *Choosing rather to suffer affliction with the people of God, than to enjoy the pleasures of sin for a season;*

Or, are you enjoying sin for a season?

Just as Moses chose to suffer, I too am a rebel *with* a cause.

Holiness or Hell?

Holiness:
To be holy is to be morally and ethically whole, to be perfect. Holiness is part of God's nature and His people are required to be holy. Holiness may be equated to godliness. You may be set aside for God's service that you do. Holiness is a way of life.

Deuteronomy 7:6
6   *For thou art an holy people unto the Lord thy God: the Lord thy God hath chosen thee to be a special people unto himself, above all people that are upon the face of the earth.*

Hell:
Hell is the place of eternal punishment for the unrighteous. There are different words used to describe the place.

In Jewish, Christian, and Islamic scripture, Gehenna is a destination of the wicked. This is different from the more neutral Sheol/Hades, the abode of the dead. In the King James Version of the Bible, each word is translated using the word "Hell."

"Hades" in Christian theology (New Testament Greek) is parallel to Hebrew word, "Sheol," meaning grave or dirt pit, and refers to the abode of the dead.

Sermon Outline

At a church convention, when many churches gather together to praise and worship, you hear different preachers preach on holiness. You hear everyone speak about the difference between the church of years ago and how it is today. Those old preachers could really preach. My question, though, is: If they were really good sermons and preachers, then why are you not living holy?

Don't forget.
Lights Out at Midnight.

Biblical Holiness.

Leviticus 11:44-45
44   For I am the Lord your God: ye shall therefore sanctify yourselves, and ye shall be holy; for I am holy: neither shall ye defile yourselves with any manner of creeping thing that creepeth upon the earth.
45   For I am the Lord that bringeth you up out of the land of Egypt, to be your God: ye shall therefore be holy, for I am holy.

You have heard preachers teach on Biblical Holiness. We all know that holiness is a way of life. "Be ye holy for I am holy." Living holy is not just a Sunday morning display.

Matthew 25:10-13
10   And while they went to buy, the bridegroom came; and they that were ready went in with him to the marriage: and the door was shut.

11   Afterward came also the other virgins, saying, Lord, Lord, open to us.
12   But he answered and said, Verily I say unto you, I know you not.
13   Watch therefore, for ye know neither the day nor the hour wherein the Son of man cometh.

As verse 13 says, you know not the time. It could be Thursday or Friday night while you're at the club. Here He comes!

The Bridegroom comes. The door is shut. Lord, Lord, open to us. I know you not. Watch. Watch out!

Lights Out at Midnight.
Holiness or Hell?

If you are like the man in the glass (mirror) that James talks about, you are deceiving your own selves.

James 1:22-24
22   But be ye doers of the word, and not hearers only, deceiving your own selves.
23   For if any be a hearer of the word, and not a doer, he is like unto a man beholding his natural face in a glass:
24   For he beholdeth himself, and goeth his way, and straightway forgeteth what manner of man he was.

Lights Out at Midnight.
Holiness or Hell?

Since you think that you know all there is to know about holiness, let me talk to you about hell.

Hell is the final abode of the unrighteous dead wherein the ungodly suffer eternal punishment. Some of you believe that hell is not real. Some of you believe that heaven is real but not hell.

Gehenna – final punishment

Luke 12:1-5
1   In the mean time, when there were gathered together an innumerable multitude of people, insomuch that they trode one upon another, he began to say unto his disciples first of all, Beware ye of the leaven of the Pharisees, which is hypocrisy.
2   For there is nothing covered, that shall not be revealed; neither hid, that shall not be known.
3   Therefore whatsoever ye have spoken in darkness shall be heard in the light; and that which ye have spoken in the ear in closets shall be proclaimed upon the housetops.
4   And I say unto you my friends, Be not afraid of them that kill the body, and after that have no more that they can do.
5   But I will forewarn you whom ye shall fear: Fear him, which after he hath killed hath power to cast into hell; yea, I say unto you, Fear him.

Who has the power to determine where you are going to go? Heaven or Hell? God has the power. Fear Him and keep His commandments.

Hades, the abode of the Dead.

Luke 16:19-31
19   There was a certain rich man, which was clothed in purple and fine linen, and fared sumptuously every day:
20   And there was a certain beggar named Lazarus, which was laid at his gate, full of sores,
21   And desiring to be fed with the crumbs which fell from the rich man's table: moreover the dogs came and licked his sores.

22   And it came to pass, that the beggar died, and was carried by the angels into Abraham's bosom: the rich man also died, and was buried:
23   And in hell he lift up his eyes, being in torments, and seeth Abraham afar off, and Lazarus in his bosom.
24   And he cried and said, Father Abraham, have mercy on me, and send Lazarus, that he may dip the tip of his finger in water, and cool my tongue; for I am tormented in this flame.
25   But Abraham said, Son, remember that thou in thy lifetime receivedst thy good things, and likewise Lazarus evil things: but now he is comforted, and thou art tormented.
26   And beside all this, between up and you there is a great gulf fixed: so that they which would pass from hence to you cannot; neither can they pass to us, that would come from thence.
27   Then he said, I pray thee therefore, father, that thou wildest send him to my father's house:
28   For I have five brethren; that he may testify unto them, lest they also come into this place of torment.
29   Abraham saith unto him, They have Moses and the prophets; let them hear them.
30   And he said, Nay, Father Abraham: but if one went unto them from the dead, they will repent.
31   And he said unto him, If they hear not Moses and the prophets, neither will they be persuaded though one rose from the dead.

There's a great gulf with no water. Only flames tormenting. All of the things a rich man was not used to. Yet he was a churchgoing man, every Sunday, but like the five foolish, he did not know when the bridegroom was coming.

Remember,
Lights Out at Midnight.

The old time preachers, they didn't help. Paul's letters didn't help. Peter's sermons didn't work. Jesus dying on the cross didn't stop hell from enlarging itself. Coming up to meet you, what would make you think Lazarus dipping his finger in the water would save you, rich man, church goer, from going to hell?

2 Peter 2:4
4   For if God spared not the angels that sinned, but cast them down to hell, and delivered them into chains of darkness, to be reserved unto judgment;

What makes a man hell-bound?

2 Peter 2:14,18
14   Having eyes full of adultery, and that cannot cease from sin; beguiling unstable souls: an heart they have exercised with covetous practices; cursed children:
18   For when they speak great swelling words of vanity, they allure through the lusts of the flesh, through much wantonness, those that were clean escaped from them who live in error.

Then, Proverbs 6:16-19 says,

Proverbs 6:16-19
16   These six things doth the Lord hate: yea, seven are an abomination unto him:
17   A proud look, a lying tongue, and hands that shed innocent blood,
18   An heart that deviseth wicked imaginations, feet that be swift in running to mischief,
19   A false witness that speaketh lies, and he that soweth discord among brethren.

Heaven or hell? The choice is yours. The door was open to the five wise with heaven in view. To the five foolish, the door was shut, with Hell enlarging itself.

Remember,
> **Lights Out at Midnight.**

Watch

Pay attention to what is going on around you. You've got to be watchful. Remember the hope that is in within. Remember the grace of God that abounds within you. The Holy Ghost is going to keep you in remembrance.

Pay close attention to the Word of God. You do not know the time or the hour when the Son of God will come. Make enough preparation to go beyond the appointed hour, just in case God doesn't come when He's supposed to.

We need to live in expectation of the Lord's return.

Sermon Outline

Watch – **Lights Out at Midnight**.

Matthew 25:13
13   Watch therefore, for ye know neither the day nor the hour werein the Son of man cometh.

Now God…grace that is given to me of God.

Roman 15:13-15
13   Now the God of hope fill you with all joy and peace in believing, that ye may abound in hope, through the power of the Holy Ghost.
14   And I myself also am persuaded of you, my brethren, that ye also are full of goodness, filled with all knowledge, able also to admonish one another.
15   Nevertheless, brethren, I have written the more boldly unto you in some sort, as putting you in mind, because of the grace that is given to me of God,

Joy. You believe that you are full of joy. This joy I have the world did give it to me…

Joy in the Holy Ghost. Not meat and drink but righteousness.

Romans 14:17
17   For the kingdom of God is not meat and drink; but righteousness, and peace, and joy in the Holy Ghost.

Peace.

The Gospel of Ephesians 6:15
15   And your feet shod with the preparation of the gospel of peace;

Beautiful feet; sexy feet. Why? Because they are prepared to bring the Gospel.

Isaiah 52:7
7   How beautiful upon the mountains are the feet of him that bringeth good tidings, that publisheth peace; that bringeth good tidings of good, that publisheth salvation; that sayith unto Zion, Thy God reigneth!

Abounding Hope. The hope that is in you. Be ready to answer the call – about your abounding hope. God sees you. I am watching too.

You are full of goodness. You are filled with knowledge. You are able to admonish one another.

1 Peter 3:15 – from the Holy Spirit
15   But sanctify the Lord God in your hearts: and be ready always to give an answer to every man that asketh you a reason of the hope that is in you with meekness and fear:

Personal Grace. A wedding, five wise virgins, five foolish. God has the key and the door was shut.

Matthew 25:1-13
1   Then shall the kingdom of heaven be likened unto ten virgins, which took their lamps, and went forth to meet the bridegroom.
2   And five of them were wise, and five were foolish.

*3	They that were foolish took their lamps, and took no oil with them:*
*4	but the wise took oil in their vessels with their lamps.*
*5	While the bridegroom tarried, they all slumbered and slept.*
*6	And at midnight there was a cry made, Behold, the bridegroom cometh; go ye out to meet him.*
*7	Then all those virgins arose, and trimmed their lamps.*
*8	And the foolish said unto the wise, Give us of your oil; for our lamps are gone out.*
*9	but the wise answered, saying, Not so; lest there be not enough for us and you: but go ye rather to them that sell, and buy for yourselves.*
*10	And while they went to buy, the bridegroom came; and they that were ready went in with him to the marriage: and the door was shut.*
*11	Afterward came also the other virgins, saying, Lord, Lord, open to us.*
*12	But he answered and said, Verily I say unto you, I know you not.*
*13	Watch therefore, for ye know neither the day nor the hour wherein the Son of man cometh.*

God is telling all of us to watch over our soul. We don't know not just when the bridegroom cometh. He isn't just some groom but He is the Son of God. Watch and enjoy your life in Christ Jesus.

Lights Out at Midnight.

Part II:
Romance & Relationships

Charge It to My Account

If you're anything like me (Laura), then you passed over the Book of Philemon, never realizing it was there. It comes just before the Book of Hebrews and was written by Paul as a letter to his friend, Philemon, on behalf of Onesimus. It contains only one chapter.

Philemon was a wealthy Christian who lived in Colossae. He hosted a church in his house. Paul converted Philemon. The Book of Philemon tells of Onesimus, who is a runaway slave of Philemon. Onesimus stole and damaged Philemon's property and ranaway to Rome, where he met Paul and was converted, as well. Paul writes to Philemon to ask him to forgive Onesimus and set him free.

Philemon owes Paul a lot more, since they were partners in finding the Lord. Paul is begging Philemon to consider Onesimus an extension of himself, so that he may be pardoned for any wrongdoing he may have caused.

Sermon Outline

The subject is Charge It based on the use of your charge card. At Christmas time, people start to pull out their charge cards or gift cards. Charge It!

Paul even used a charge card in Philemon 18, "Put that on my account." Paul is making a request, or a purchase. He is requesting that Philemon act differently with Onesimus. Paul is buying his pardon or his release. Paul and Philemon have a relationship in Christ Jesus. Because of this partnership, he wants him to hear his plea. As partners in crime or in marriage, the request is made on my behalf. Receive him as myself.

If Onesimus had wronged thee, or if he owes you anything, put this debt on my account.

Jesus paid it all – one more thing, as the old song said, "What more could He do?" Open up your heart. There is room for you at the cross.

Jesus has paid the price on Calvary. He paid it all. What more do you want him to do? All you have to do is be willing to charge it to Him. He's willing.

Song: "What more can I do? He laid the foundation. He opened up the way. What more can He do?"

Jesus is willing to act on our behalf. He died on the cross for us. The relationship you have with your partner cannot replace the relationship you have with Jesus.

Philemon 1:17-19
17   If thou count me therefore a partner, receive him as myself.

18   If he hath wronged thee, or oweth thee ought, put that on mine account;
19   I Paul have written it with mine own hand. I will repay it: albeit I do not say to thee how thou owest unto me even tine own self besides.

Charge It to My Account: whatever Onesimus owed – I'll pay. Remember, Jesus paid it all. Remember your own sin debt. He is asking Philemon to liberate Onesimus.

Ain't Got No Problem

This sermon is a continuation of Charge It To My Account.

Each of us has a choice. We can either dwell on our problems, or look to God for solutions. The choice is ours.

Paul is the most influential Christian and one of the earliest teachers of Jesus' teachings.

In Philemon, he is requesting that Onesimus be considered as an extension of himself. We are all extensions of God. Through the teachings of Jesus Christ, we know that He is writing on our behalf, just like Paul did for Onesimus.

Sermon Outline

We talked about Philemon in the sermon, "Charge It to My Account." We looked specifically at Philemon 1:17-19, where Paul is requesting of Philemon to consider Onesimus as if he were an extension of Paul. He is asking Philemon to liberate him.

This sermon is going to look at Philemon 1:20-21.

Philemon 1:20-21
20   Yea, brother, let me have joy of thee in the Lord: refresh my bowels in the Lord.
21   Having confidence in thy obedience I wrote unto thee, knowing that thou will do more than I say.

Only Paul's letter to Philemon is recorded in the Bible. Philemon's response is not included. I am sure that Philemon answered Paul by saying, "Ain't got no problem." No problem at all – Onesimus is forgiven.

First giving honor to God, I have preached your Word, O God.

Psalms 40:8-10
8   I delight to do thy will, O my God: yea, thy law is within my heart.
9   I have preached righteousness in the great congregation: lo, I have not refrained my lips, O Lord, thou knowest.
10   I have not hid thy righteousness within my heart: I have declared thy faithfulness and thy salvation: I have not concealed thy lovingkindless and thy truth from the great congregation.

Paul, I remember you.

Hebrew 13:7
7   *Remember them which have the rule over you, who have spoken unto you the word of God: whose faith follow, considering the end of their conversation.*

Yes, Paul, I remember your teaching.

Galatians 6:1-10
1   *Brethren, if a man be overtaken in a fault, ye which are spiritual, restore such an one in the spirit of meekness; considering thyself, lest thou also be tempted.*
2   *Bear ye one another's burdens, and so fulfil the law of Christ.*
3   *For if a man think himself to be something, when he is nothing, he deceiveth himself.*
4   *But let every man prove his own work, and then shall he have rejoicing in himself alone, and not in another.*
5   *For every man shall bear his own burden.*
6   *Let him that is taught in the word communicate unto him that teacheth in all good things.*
7   *Be not deceived; God is not mocked: for whatsoever a man soweth, that shall he also reap.*
8   *For he that soweth to his flesh shall of the flesh reap corruption; but he that soweth to the Spirit shall of the Spirit reap life everlasting.*
9   *And let us not be weary in well doing: for in due season we shall reap, if we faint not.*
10   *As we have therefore opportunity, let us do good unto all men, especially unto them who are of the household of faith.*

Ain't Got No Problem – Charge It

This sermon is asking the question: Is Christ living in you?

The Bible refers to both Zion and Jerusalem. They are the same city. When Jerusalem is referred to as Zion, it is the holy city in its heavenly and righteous state. God dwells in holy states.

You are also Zion, because you also can be a heavenly, righteous state. God should dwell there, within you. But that's not what is happening all the time. Sometimes, we are Jerusalem and sometimes we are Zion. We must strive to be Zion, in our righteous, holy state, all the time.

Think about what is around you. When you are at church. What's the matter? Are you in your righteous, holy state at church? Do you just go to church because that is what you are supposed to do?

When you eat, are you just eating to satisfy your own hunger, or are you in your heavenly, righteous state? Is eating a special occasion, like Communion or the Love Feast to remember God and Jesus in a sacred way? Do you give thanks? Is it the Lord's supper your own supper?

Sermon Outline

Can we answer, "Ain't got no problem – Charge it" to those who ask of us?

We sing: "O Zion what the matter now? We don't sing like we used we used to sing, pray, shout, and the list goes on. O Zion, what the matter now?"

Isaiah 1:21
21 How is the faithful city become an harlot! It was full of judgment; righteousness lodged in it; but now murderers.

Tell us the problem. Our city is but a harlot. Zion, you were full of judgment and righteousness, but now you are full of murderers.

Zion, we got a problem. Let's go back a few verses.

Isaiah 1:18-20
18 Come now, and let us reason together, saith the Lord: though your sins be as scarlet, they shall be as white as snow; though they be red like crimson, they shall be as wool.
19 If ye be willing and obedient, ye shall eat the good of the land:
20 But if ye refuse and rebel, ye shall be devoured with the sword: for the mouth of the Lord hath spoken it.

Come <u>now</u> and let us reason together. Verse 19 states the problem. If you are <u>willing</u> and <u>obedient</u>, then you shall eat the good of the land.

Zion could answer, "Ain't got no problem – Charge It," but in verse 20, if you <u>refuse</u> and <u>rebel</u>, then you will be devoured.

God, we got a problem. In the story of the "Love Feast," there is lack of love. Paul tries to restore dignity at the meal. Paul reminds us that there are symbols of divine love. Paul says, "Let a man examine himself…"

1 Corinthians 11:28
28   But let a man examine himself, and so let him eat of the bread, and drink of that cup.

Jesus Christ is in me. I can say it, and you can say it, too. Ain't got no problem.

2 Corinthians 13:5
5   Examine yourselves, whether ye be in the faith; prove your own selves. Know ye not your own selves, how that Jesus Christ is in you, except ye be reprobates?

Yes, Paul send Onesimus home. Ain't got no problem.
Jesus paid it all! Just like Paul plead for Onesimus' life; Jesus has died for your life. Just Charge It – Ain't no problem, the debt is paid in full.

Sexy Feet

Why are we talking about beautiful and sexy feet? Because they are prepared to bring the Gospel.

Isaiah 52:7
7   How beautiful upon the mountains are the feet of him that bringeth good tidings, that publisheth peace; that bringeth good tidings of good, that publisheth salvation; that saith unto Zion, Thy God reigneth!

Sexy feet are the appealing and exciting side of Word of God, in which a man and woman must stand on and build their relationship and marriage. How sexy or attractive is that!

How do you know you have sexy feet? There are four points that will show you that have sexy feet:
1. Bring good tidings.
2. Publish peace.
3. Bring good tidings of good.
4. Publish salvation.

Sermon Outline

Let's look at these points that help show us our Sexy Feet.

Bring Good Tidings
Jesus taught us in Matthew 5:14 saying God is the light of the world, compared to a city on a hill that always stands out.

Matthew 5:14
14   Ye are the light of the world. A city that is set on an hill cannot be hid.

Yes, Sexy Feet bring good tidings.

Matthew 5:16
16   Let your light shine before men, that they may see your good works, and glorify your Father which is in heaven.

Yes, Sexy Feet that bring good tidings. As Jesus told us, rise and stand on your feet for I (Jesus Christ) have appeared for this purpose, to MAKE you sanctified by the faith that IS IN ME.

Acts 26:16 & 18
16   But rise, and stand upon thy feet: for I have appeared unto thee for this purpose, to make thee a minister and a witness both of these things which thou hast seen, and of those things in which I will appear unto thee;

18   To open their eyes, and to turn them from darkness to light, and from the power of Satan unto God, that they make receive forgiveness of sins, and inheritance among them which are sanctified by faith that is in me.

Publish Peace

When you publish something, you prepare and issue a message. You communicate. In the scriptures on the Sermon the Mount, Jesus blesses the peacemakers. Yes, my Sexy Feet are causing peace. This message must be published. I am a peacemaker!

Matthew 5:9

9   Blessed are the peacemakers: for they shall be called the children of God.

Sometimes, we feel no love, have no righteousness within us, and there's no one who chastises us. Have we forgotten what we knew as a child?

Hebrews 12:5-10

5   And ye have forgotten the exhortation which speaketh unto you as unto children, My son, despise not thou the chastening of the Lord, nor faint when thou art rebuked of him:
6   For whom the Lord loveth he chasteneth, and scourgeth every son whom he receiveth.
7   If ye endure chastening, God dealeth with you as with sons; for what son is he whom the father chasteneth not?
8   But if ye be without chastisement, whereof all are partakers, then are ye bastards, and not sons.
9   Furthermore we have had fathers of our flesh which corrected us, and we have them reverence: shall we not much rather be in subjection unto the Father of spirits, and live?

10   For they verily for a few days chastened us after their own pleasure; but he for our profit, that we might be partakers of his holiness.

To have Sexy Feet, you MUST bring forth peace and publish holiness with your words and actions.

Matthew 5:11-14
11   Blessed are ye, when men shall revile you, and persecute you, and shall say all manner of evil against you falsely, for my sake.
12   Rejoice, and be exceeding glad: for great is your reward in heaven: for so persecuted they the prophets which were before you.
13   Ye are the salt of the earth: if the salt have lost his savour, wherewith shall it be salted? It is thenceforth good for nothing, but to be cast out, and to be trodden under foot of men.
14   Ye are the light of the world. A city that is set on an hill cannot be hid.

Bring Good Tidings of Good
We have already talked about bringing good tidings. Now, we will talk about good tidings of good. So what is good?

We must bring tidings of good, or the gospel to all nations. We must evangelize.

Mark 13:10
10   And the gospel must first be published among all nations.

The Gospel is not just about words alone, but the power of the Holy Ghost. Act in accordance with the Gospel.

Philippians 1:27
27   Only let your conversation be as it becometh the gospel of Christ: that whether I come and see you, or else be absent, I may hear of your affairs, that ye stand fast in one spirit, with one mine striving together for the faith of the gospel.

Publish Salvation
Remember that publish means to prepare, issue, or communicate. Before my old, dead feet got to be Sexy Feet, I waited patiently for the Lord.

Psalm 40:1
1   I waited patiently for the Lord; and he inclined unto e, and heard my cry.

To be published, I had to wait on the Lord, then He communicated with me. He heard my godly cry. In order to get Sexy Feet, you have to want to have Sexy Feet.

Psalm 40:2
2   He brought me up also out of an horrible pit, out of the miry clay, and set my feet upon a rock, and established my goings.

My feet were old and dead, but He brought me up. Jesus Christ made me stand on the solid rock, His foundation, then the Holy Spirit established in me good tidings, published peace, and received good tidings of good, or the Gospel.

Praise God, Praise God, my <u>Sexy Feet</u> help me to walk upright and stand on the Word of God.

Ephesians 6:15
15   And your feet shod with the preparation of the gospel of peace;

Yes, you too can have Sexy Feet.

1 Samuel 2:9a
9   He will keep the feet of his saints, and the wicked shall be silent in darkness; for by strength shall no man prevail.

God the Father, God the Son and God the Holy Spirit will keep your feet beautiful and SEXY. Ya, sexy feet!!!

The Love of God

Is God's Love conditional or unconditional? For one thing, God loves *all* of His children. This includes you, dear reader. He holds us in highest regard, just the way we should hold our fellow brothers and sisters.

Psalm 17:7
7   *Show thy marvelous lovingkindness, O thou that savest by thy right hand them which put their trust in thee from those that rise up against them.*

Love is referenced in the Bible hundreds of times. But nothing compares to God's unconditional love for His Son, Jesus Christ, who died on the Cross.

John 3:16
16   *For God so loved the world, that he have his only begotten Son, that whosoever believeth in him should not perish, but have everlasting life.*

Sermon Outline

The Love of God can be shown in several ways:
1. Communication
2. Marriage
3. Discipleship
4. Love

Note: Each can be done as their own sermon if you choose.

GOD'S LOVE

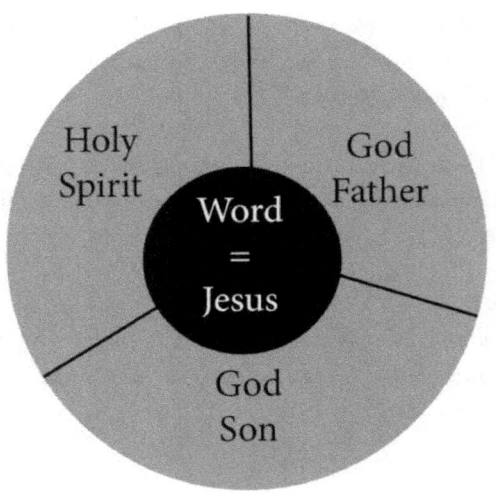

1. Communication

Revelation 3:20
20 Behold, I stand at the door; and knock: if any man hear my voice, and open the door, I will come in to him, and will sup with him, and he with me.

In this passage, "sup" means to eat with, at which time one can talk to one another. In slang, "sup" is a shortened form of "What's Up?", which is also a form of communication.

Before you can communicate with God, you first need to know his word. You must study the Word of God.

2 Timothy 2:15
15 Study to show thyself approved unto God, a workman that needeth not to be ashamed, rightly dividing the word of truth.

You can find His Word by reading His Book, the Bible.

2 Timothy 3:16-17
16 All scripture is given by inspiration of God, and is profitable for doctrine, for reproof, for correction, for instruction in righteousness:
17 That the man of God may be perfect, thoroughly furnished unto all good works.

Now God and you can communicate. As Paul says, read it for yourself.

1 Corinthians 2:1-16

1 And I, brethren, when I came to you, came not with excellency of speech or of wisdom, declaring unto you the testimony of God.

2 For I determined not to know any thing among you, save Jesus Christ, and him crucified.

3 And I was with you in weakness, and in fear, and in much trembling.

4 And my speech and my preaching was not with enticing words of man's wisdom, but in demonstration of the Spirit and of power:

5 That your faith should not stand in the wisdom of men, but in the power of God.

6 Howbeit we speak wisdom among them that are perfect: yet not the wisdom of this world, nor of the princes of this world, that come to nought:

7 But we speak with the wisdom of God in a mystery, even the hidden wisdom, which God ordained before the world unto our glory.

8 Which none of the princes of this world knew: for had they known it, they would not have crucified the Lord of glory.

9 But as it is written, Eye hath not seen, nor ear heard, neither have entered into the heart of man, the things which God hath prepared for them that love him.

10 But God hath revealed them unto us by his Spirit: for the Spirit searcheth all things, yea, the deep things of God.

11 For what man knoweth the things of a man, save the spirit of man which is in him? Even so the things of God knoweth no man, but the Spirit of God.

12 Now we had received, not the spirit of the world, but the spirit which is God; that we might know the things that are freely given to us of God.

13   Which things also we speak, not in the words which man's wisdom teacheth, but which the Holy Ghost teacheth; comparing spiritual things with spiritual.
14   But the natural man receiveth not the things of the Spirit of God: for they are foolishness unto him: neither can he know them, because they are spiritually discerned.
15   But he that is spiritual judgeth all things, yet he himself is judged of no man.
16   For who hath known the mind of the Lord, that he may instruct him? But we have the mind of Christ.

In 1 Corinthians 2:12, now we have received the spirit of God.

1 Corinthians 2:12
12   Now we had received, not the spirit of the world, but the spirit which is God; that we might know the things that are freely given to us of God.

In 1 Corinthians 2:13, by the teaching of the Holy Spirit, let us speak using God's words.

1 Corinthians 2:13
13   Which things also we speak, not in the words which man's wisdom teacheth, but which the Holy Ghost teacheth; comparing spiritual things with spiritual.

In 1 Corinthian 2:14, the natural man cannot communicate with God.

1 Corinthians 2:14
14   But the natural man receiveth not the things of the Spirit of God: for they are foolishness unto him: neither can he know them, because they are spiritually discerned.

In 1 Corinthians 2:15, but he that is spiritual judges all things.

1 Corinthians 2:15
15   But he that is spiritual judgeth all things, yet he himself is judged of no man.

In 1 Corinthians 2:16, why? Because the spiritual man has the mind of Christ.

1 Corinthians 2:16
16   For who hath known the mind of the Lord, that he may instruct him? But we have the mind of Christ.

When I first started to communicate with God, after salvation, and after studying and receiving the mind of Christ, I wrote letters to God. I would write:

Dear God;
I would date it and write my thoughts, feelings, and wants into the letter. I would end it with thank you. Then, I would place the letter in my Family Bible.

I continued to write letters to God. Then, after a year or two, I would reread the letters, and date my reread, thanking God for answering, sometimes updating the request or canceling it.

Of course, I communicated through prayer, daily chats, reading, and studying God's word. When thinking about daily chats, remember Genesis 3:8, when God walks through the garden and talks to Adam.

Genesis 3:8
8   And they heard the voice of the Lord God walking in the garden in the cool of the day: and Adam and his wife hid themselves from the presence of the Lord God amongst the trees of the garden.

God's messages/communication are always truth, joy and love.

God's Message #1: Truth
Truth is the chief cornerstone of all of God's statements. In the beginning, Truth created the world.

Genesis 1:1
1   In the beginning God created the heaven and the earth.

And in the end, a great multitude was heard.

Revelation 19:6
6   And I heard as it were the voice of a great multitude, and as the voice of many waters, and as the voice of mighty thunderings, saying Alleluia: for the Lord God omnipotent reigneth.

And He said, Write, for these words are true and faithful.

Revelation 21:5
5   And he that sat upon he throne said, Behold, I make all things new. And he said unto me, Write, for these words are true and faithful.

And he sent his angels to show us the things that are needed to be done.

Revelation 22:6
6   And he said unto me, These sayings are faithful and true: and the Lord God of the holy prophets sent his angel to show unto his servants the things which must shortly be done.

Take all you need from this book, and God will do His part.

Revelation 22:19
19   And if any man shall take away from the words of the book of this prophecy, God shall take away his part out of the book of life, and out of the holy city, and form the things which are written in this book.

Truth is Jesus Christ: Read John 14: 6-21.
[Editor's Note: You can find these verses in the appendix]

Truth is the Holy Spirit: Read John 16:5-14.
[Editor's Note: You can find these verses in the appendix]

Rightly divide the word of truth. Remember in 2 Timothy 2:15, you are advised to study the world of truth.

2 Timothy 2:15
2   Study to show thyself approved unto God, a workman that needeth not to be ashamed, rightly dividing the word of truth.

Why? So you can rightly divide the word of truth. This is how you communicate with God. Then, you can communicate with others by preaching the power of God.

2 Timothy 4:1-5
1   *I charge thee therefore before God, and the Lord Jesus Christ, who shall judge the quick and the dead at his appearing and his kingdom;*
2   *Preach the word; be instant in season, out of season; reprove, rebuke, exhort with all longsuffering and doctrine.*
3   *For the time will come when they will not endure sound doctrine; but after their own lusts shall they heap to themselves teachers, having itching ears;*
4   *And they shall turn away their ears from the truth, and shall be turned unto fables.*
5   *But watch thou in all things, endure afflictions, do the work of an evangelist, make full proof of thy ministry.*

God's Message #2: Joy

Psalm 43 speaks of God as exceeding great joy. Verse 3 reminds us to communicate that Jesus is the light and truth.

Psalm 43:3
3   *O send out thy light and thy truth: let them lead me; let them bring me unto thy holy hill, and to thy tabernacles.*

God is my exceeding joy, and I will praise Him.

Psalm 43:4
4   *Then I will go unto the altar of God, unto God my exceeding joy: yea, upon the harp will I praise thee, O God my God.*

Joy is God. My exceeding great joy is God. To have joy, you must have God. Ask your soul a question. Why?

Psalm 43:5
5   Why art thou cast down, O my soul? and why art thou disquieted within me? hope in God: for I shall yet praise him, who is the health of my countenance, and my God.

I still have joy! "I still have JOY…" is one of my favorite songs. "After all everything I been through I still have joy." To still have joy, you must know God! A song is just a song, and words are just words; to have JOY, you've got to know God. There must be some communication with God going on in order to be joyful.
My soul is built on hope. To have joy, my soul built is on a hope.

Titus 2:13
13   Looking for that blessed hope, and the glorious appearing of the great God and our Saviour Jesus Christ;

Yes, "After all, after all everything I been through," anticipating hope, I still have JOY!

God's Message #3: Love
The greatest of all of God's messages is Love. Charity is Love.

1 Corinthians 13:13
13   And now abideth faith, hope, charity, these three; but the greatest of these is charity.

For God so loved. "So Loved" means more than a single moment in time. This love is continuous and constant.

John 3:16
16   For God so loved the world, that he gave his own begotten Son, that whosoever believeth in him should not perish, but have everlasting life.

Yes, God gave us His son, Jesus.

John 15:13-14
13   Greater love hath no man than this, that a man lay down his life for his friends.
14   Ye are my friends, if ye do whatsoever I command you.

Jesus laid down His life for us on Calvary and rose again to confirm His love by sitting on the right of God.

Hebrews 12:2
2   Looking unto Jesus the author and finisher of our faith; who for the joy that was set before him endured the cross, despising the shame, and is set down at the right hand of the throne of God.

Romans 8:34
34   Who is he that condemneth? It is Christ that died, yea rather that is risen again, who is even at the right hand of God, who also maketh intercession for us.

Remember God is Love.

1 John 4:8
8   He that loveth not knoweth not God; for God is love.

Communication between God and you has always been based on truth; my daughter said to me one day, "Well, there is his side of the story and also her side of the story. Then, there is the Truth. Only God knows the Truth."

When you talk to God about anything, there is exceeding great Joy.
Yes, after you communicate with God, the feeling of Love overshadows and consumes you.

Try communicating with God, not just through prayer, but by walking in His garden of life on a daily basis. Make Him part of your life.

2. Marriage

Mark 10:9
9   I am the door: by me if any man enter in, he shall be saved, and shall go in and out, and find pasture.

Marriage is the bedrock of the relationship between man, woman, and God.

Genesis 2:18
18   And the Lord God said, It is not good that the man should be alone; I will make him an help meet for him.

So God created woman.

Genesis 2:21-25
21   And the Lord God caused deep sleep to fall upon Adam and he slept: and he took one of his ribs, and closed up the flesh instead thereof;
22   And the rib, which the Lord God had taken from man, made he a woman, and brought her unto the man.
23   And Adam said, This is now the bone of my bones, and flesh of my flesh: she shall be called Woman, because she was taken out of Man.
24   Therefore shall a man leave his father and his mother, and shall cleave unto his wife: and they shall be one flesh.
25   And they were both naked, the man and his wife, and were not ashamed.

We find ourselves at the foundation of marriage. The foundation is:
    1. Given by God
    2. Two Becoming One Flesh
    3. Naked

4. Not Ashamed

Let's look at each of these stones in the foundation:

Foundation Stone #1: Given by God
The Lord God is the husband, not just the head of the house, but the head of the church of God.

Isaiah 54:5
5   For thy Maker is thine husband; the Lord of hosts is his name; and the Redeemer the Holy One of Israel; The God of the whole earth shall he be called.

Read the story about the wise and foolish maidens.

Matthew 25:1-13
1   Then shall the kingdom of heaven be likened unto ten virgins, which took their lamps, and went forth to meet the bridegroom.
2   And five of them were wise, and five were foolish.
3   They that were foolish took their lamps, and took no oil with them:
4   but the wise took oil in their vessels with their lamps.
5   While the bridegroom tarried, they all slumbered and slept.
6   And at midnight there was a cry made, Behold, the bridegroom cometh; go ye out to meet him.
7   Then all those virgins arose, and trimmed their lamps.
8   And the foolish said unto the wise, Give us of your oil; for our lamps are gone out.
9   but the wise answered, saying, Not so; lest there be not enough for us and you: but go ye rather to them that sell, and buy for yourselves.

10   And while they went to buy, the bridegroom came; and they that were ready went in with him to the marriage: and the door was shut.
11   Afterward came also the other virgins, saying, Lord, Lord, open to us.
12   But he answered and said, Verily I say unto you, I know you not.
13   Watch therefore, for ye know neither the day nor the hour wherein the Son of man cometh.

God tells us who the Bride is in Matthew 25. You and I are the Bride in this story. Remember, five were wise and five were foolish. Do you have enough oil to fill up your lamp? Do you have back-up supply, just in case?

Lights Out at Midnight.

Foundation Stone #2: Two Becoming One Flesh
You and I are the Bride and we are betrothed to God, our husband. We shall become One, together in marriage.

Hosea 2:19-20
19   And I will betroth thee unto me for ever; yea, I will betroth thee unto me in righteousness, and in judgment, and in lovingkindness, and in mercies.
20   I will even betroth thee unto me in faithfulness: and thou shalt know the Lord.

Becoming one in righteousness, justice, steadfast love, mercy and faithfulness; each intertwined with the Lord/husband and the bride (you and me). You and I become one with God so that we may know each other as one until death do us part.

Romans 7:2
2   For the woman which hath an husband is bound by the law to her husband so long as he liveth; but if the husband be dead, she is loosed from the law of her husband.

Foundation Stone #3: Naked
When we think about being naked, we might think about the giving of one self, cleansing by the washing of the word, using incense in a room, or presenting oneself without spot or wrinkle. When we are naked before the Lord, we are holy without blemish, naked in our love.

Ephesians 5:25-30
25   Husbands, love your wives, even as Christ also loved the church, and gave himself for it;
26   That he might sanctify and cleanse it with the washing of water by the word,
27   That he might present it to himself a glorious church, not having spot, or wrinkle, or any such thing; but that it should be holy and without blemish.
28   So ought men to love their wives as their own bodies. He that loveth his wife loveth himself.
29   For no man ever yet hated his own flesh; but nourisheth and clerisheth it, even as the Lord the church:
30   For we are members of his body, of his flesh, and of his bones.

Foundation Stone #4: Not Ashamed

I am not ashamed. This why we leave our parents and are giving by God, becoming one flesh, naked-joined together and not ashamed in marriage – this is a great mystery!

Ephesians 5:31-33
31   For this cause shall a man leave his father and mother, and shall be joined unto his wife, and they two shall be one flesh,
32   This is the great mystery: but I speak concerning Christ and the church.
33   Nevertheless let every one of you in particular so love his wife even as himself; and the wife see that she reverence her husband.

So, we've got the foundation of marriage, now let's build on it. This marriage is then to become the foundation for a home, a family, and a life.

A Good Thing.

Proverbs 18:22
22   Whoso findeth a wife findeth a good thing, and obtaineth favour of the Lord.

Have any of you ever been married before? If you have, then you know that the bed is undefiled. What does that mean? It means to not commit adultery with another and to keep your marriage bed pure.

Hebrews 13:4
4   Marriage is honourable in all, and the bed undefiled: but whoremongers and adulterers God will judge.

The institution of marriage is given by God.

Genesis 2:24
24   Therefore shall a man leave his father and his mother, and shall cleave unto his wife: and they shall be one flesh.

Yes, the reconciliation of marriage must start with us as people who want to know and understand God's Word. God created the first marriage for the purpose of procreation, dominion over all creation, and companionship as stated in the foundational points found in Genesis.

God the creator established the covenant relationship between Him and His creation.

Read Romans 1:16-25. *[Editor's Note: You can find these verses in the appendix]*

Romans 1:19-21
19   Because that which may be known of God is manifest in them; for God hath showed it unto them.
20   For the invisible things of him from the creation of the world are clearly seen, being understood by the things that are made, even his eternal power and Godhead; so that they are without excuse:
21   Because that, when they knew God, they glorified him not as God, neither were thankful; but became vain in their imaginations, and their foolish heart was darkened.

And this passage in Romans explains why marriage out in the world doesn't even look the way it used to. It has become vain in their imaginations. Therefore, as verse 21b says, "… their foolish heart was darkened." And as verse 22 states, "Professing themselves to be wise, they became fools."

Marriage is an institution and covenant created and established by God.

Matthew 19:3-6
3 The Pharisees also came unto him, tempting him, and saying unto him, Is is lawful for a man to put away his wife for every cause?
4 And he answered and said unto them, Have ye not read, that he which made them at the beginning made them male and female,
5 And said, For this cause shall a man leave father and other, and shall cleave to his wife: and they twain shall be one flesh?
6 Wherefore they are no more twain, but one flesh. What therefore God hath joined together, let not man put asunder.

Let not man put asunder.

3. Discipleship

There is a song that says, "Leaving all to follow Jesus, trusting in His holy word…" WOW! That's what discipleship is all about: leaving *all* to follow Jesus. Matthew, chapter 16 speaks of several discussion points regarding discipleship. Read Matthew 16:1-28.

Matthew 16:1-28
1   The Pharisees also with the Sadducees came, and tempting desired him that he would show them a sign from heaven.
2   He answered and said unto them, When it is evening, ye say, It will be fair weather: for the sky is red.
3   And in the morning, It will be foul weather to day: for the sky is red and lowering. O ye hypocrites, ye can discern the face of the sky; but can ye not discern the signs of the time?
4   A wicked and adulterous generation seeketh after a sign; and there shall no sign be given unto it, but the sign of the prophet Jonas. And he left them, and departed.
5   And when his disciples were come to the other side, they had forgotten to take bread.
6   Then Jesus said unto them, Take heed and beware of the leaven of the Pharisees of the Sadducees.
7   And they reasoned among themselves, saying, It is because we have taken no bread.
8   Which when Jesus perceived, he said unto them, O ye of little faith, why reason ye among yourselves, because ye have brought no bread?
9   Do ye not yet understand, neither remember the five loaves of the five thousand, and how many baskets ye took up?
10   Neither the seven loaves of the four thousand, and how many baskets ye took up?

11   How is it that ye do not understand that I spake it not to you concerning bread, that ye should beware of the leaven of the Pharisees and of the Sadducees?
12   Then understood they how that he bade them not beware of the leaven of bread, but of the doctrine of the Pharisees and of the Sadducees.
13   When Jesus came into the coasts of Caesarea Philippi, he asked his disciples, saying, Whom do men say that I the Son of man am?
14   And they said, Some say that thou art John the Baptist: some, Elias; and others, Jeremias, or one of the prophets.
15   He saith unto the, But whom say ye that I am?
16   And Simon Peter answered and said, Thou art the Christ, the Son of the living God.
17   And Jesus answered and said unto him, Blessed art thou, Simon Barjona: for flesh and blood hath not revealed it unto thee, but my Father which is in heaven.
18   And I say also unto thee, That thou art Peter, and upon this rock I will build my church; and the gates of hell shall not prevail against it.
19   And I will give unto thee that keys of the kingdom of heaven: and whatsoever thou shalt bind on earth shall be bound in heaven: and whatsoever thou shalt bind on earth shall be bound in heaven: and whatsoever thou shalt loose on earth shall be loosed in heaven.
20   Then charged he his disciples that they should tell no man that he was Jesus the Christ.
21   From that time forth began Jesus to show unto his disciples, how that he must go unto Jerusalem, and suffer many things of the elders and chief priests and scribes, and be killed, and be raised again the third day.
22   Then Peter took him, and began to rebuke him, saying, Be it far from thee, Lord: this shall not be unto thee.

23   But he turned, and said unto Peter, Get thee behind me, Satan: thou art an offence unto me: for thou savourest not the things that be of God, but those that be of men.
24   Then said Jesus unto his disciples, If any man will come after me, let him deny himself, and take up his cross, and follow me.
25   For whatsoever will save his life shall lose it: and whatsoever will lose his life for my sake shall find it.
26   For what is a man profited, if he shall gain the whole world, and lose his own soul? or what shall a man give in exchange for his soul?
27   For the Son of man shall come in the glory of his Father with his angels; and then he shall reward every man according to his works.
28   Verily I say unto you, There be some standing here, which shall not taste of death, till they see the Son of man coming in his kingdom.

1. Following Sign – Sign Seeker   vs. 1-4
2. Following of the Pharisees and Sadducees – Leaven Bread   vs. 5-12
3. Who was Jesus? – Peter's Statement vs. 13-20
4. Peter rebukes Jesus – Jesus says, "Get thee behind me, Satan…"   vs. 21-23

The above concerns should lead to true discipleship. Jesus asks his disciples in Matthew 16:24 to follow him.

Matthew 16:24
24   Then said Jesus unto his disciples, If any man will come after me, let him deny himself, and take up his cross, and follow me.

There have been many discipleship movement around (you can go online and find them); but the simplest one to follow is to follow Jesus, as stated above Matt. 16:24.

Jesus invites us to follow him in four simple steps:

- **Come after me:** Just follow Jesus.
- **Let him deny himself:** Let go and let God.
- **Take up his cross:** must Jesus bear the cross alone and all the whole go free.
- **Follow me:** Jesus is the answer for the world today.

We can follow Jesus in four simple steps, but we must play a major role in following Jesus.

Luke 14: 25-33 tell us, what is required of who want to be Christ's disciple:

Luke 14:25-33
25   And there went great multitudes with him: and he turned, and said unto them,
26   If any man come to me, and hate not his father, and mother, and wife, and children, and brethren, and sisters, yea, and his own life also, he cannot be my disciple.
27   And whosoever doth not bear his cross, and come after me, cannot be my disciple.
28   For which of you, intending to build a tower, sitteth not down first, and coutheth the cost, whether he have sufficient to finish it?
29   Lest haply, after he hath laid the foundation, and is not able to finish it, all that behold it begin to mock him,
30   Saying, This man began to build, and was not able to finish.

31   Or what king, going to make war against another king, sitteth not down first, and consulteth whether he be able with then thousand to meet him that cometh against him with twenty thousand?
32   Or else, while the other is yet a great way off, he sendeth an ambassage, and desireth conditions of peace.
33   So, likewise, whosoever he be of you that forsaketh not all that he hath, he cannot be my disciple.

Discipleship Step #1: Come after Me

Look at Luke, chapter 14, verses 26-27 in the passage above. They are listed here, too:

26   If any man come to me, and hate not his father, and mother, and wife, and children, and brethren, and sisters, yea, and his own life also, he cannot be my disciple.
27   And whosoever doth not bear his cross, and come after me, cannot be my disciple.

How can you hate your own family and yourself? Remember God gave His only begotten son! Hating your own family and self is huge cross to bear. Self-denial is a great problem for most of us. But in verse 33, Jesus says to us: If you aren't willing to take what is dearest to you and let it go, then you can't be my disciple.

Luke 14:33
33   So, likewise, whosoever he be of you that forsaketh not all that he hath, he cannot be my disciple.

Giving up family may come easy for some, but difficult for others. Denying self can come easy for some, and hard for others. Self-denial leads us to next step.

Discipleship Step #2: Let Him Deny Himself

Let Him Deny Himself is a cost factor in discipleship. My favorite scripture is Galatians 2:20.

Galatians 2:20
20   I am crucified with Christ: nevertheless I live; not I, but Christ liveth in me: and the life which I now live in the flesh I live by the faith of the Son of God, who loved me, and gave himself for me.

The word crucified means bearing my own cross. The self, or the flesh, must be crucified. It must die. This also goes for our ego.

In Galatians 5:17, Paul tells us that the Self, or flesh, and life in Christ Jesus, or Spirit, are at war and contrary to one another.

Galatians 5:17
17   For the flesh lusteth against the Spirit, and the Spirit against the flesh: and these are contrary the one to the other: so that ye cannot do the things that ye would.

Self- denial is truly a large cost, and the war between flesh and Spirit is an ongoing battle. God, just as He was with Jesus, will not be with us. Instead, He will be in us, just as He was with Jesus on the cross.

"Must Jesus bear the cross and all the world go free."

Romans 8:13-16
13   For if ye live after the flesh, ye shall die: but if ye through the Spirit do mortify the deeds of the body, ye shall live.
14   For as many as are led by the Spirit of God, they are the sons of God.
15   For ye have not received the spirit of bondage again to fear; but ye have received the Spirit of adoption, whereby we cry, Abba, Father.
16   The Spirit itself beareth witness with our spirit, that we are the children of God:

The answer in the song says, "No, there is a cross for everyone." The next step is "Take up your cross."

Discipleship Step #3: Take Up Your Cross
This is where life gets interesting. At the cross, where I first saw the light, things changed. My whole life changed. The cross is a symbol of both life and death. It represents both the death of the old man, or your old self before Christ Jesus, and the life of the new man, or your new self, in Christ Jesus.

Old things pass away, and behold all things become new. Wow! Chapter 7 in the Book of Romans talks about the old man who can't break away from sin, who has no hope. God, through the cross of Jesus Christ, makes peace and reconciles all things.

Read Romans 7:1-25.

Romans 7:1-25
1   Know ye not, brethren, (for I speak to them that know the law,) how that the law hath dominion over a man as long as he liveth?

2   For the woman which hath an husband is bound by the law to her husband so long as he liveth; but if the husband be dead, she is loosed from the law of her husband.
3   So then if, while her husband liveth, she be married to another man, she shall be called an adulteress: but if her husband be dead, she is free from that law: so that she is no adulteress, though she be married to another man.
4   Wherefore, my brethren, ye also are dead to the law by the body of Christ; that he should be married to another, even to him who is raised from the dead, that we should bring forth fruit unto God.
5   For when we were in the flesh, the motions of sins, which were by the law, did work in our members to bring forth fruit unto death.
6   But now we are delivered from the law, that being dead wherein we were held; that we should serve in newness of spirit, and not in the oldness of the letter.
7   What shall we say then? Is the law sin? God forbid. Nay, I had not known sin, but by the law: for I had not known lust, except the law had said, Thou shalt not covet.
8   But sin, taking occasion by the commandment, wrought in me all manner of concupiscence. For without the law sin was dead.
9   For I was alive without the law once: but when the commandment came, sin revived, and I died.
10   And the commandment, which was ordained to life, I found to be undo death.
11   For sin, taking occasion by the commandment, deceived me, and by it slew me.
12   Wherefore the law is holy, and the commandment holy, and just, and good.

13   Was then that which is good made death unto me? God forbid. But sin, that is might appear sin, working death in me by that which is good; that sin by the commandment might become exceeding sinful.
14   For we know that the law is spiritual: but I am carnal, sold under sin.
15   For that which I do I allow not: for what I would, that do I not; but what I hate, that do I.
16   If then I do that which I would not, I consent unto the law that it is good.
17   Now then it is no more I that do it, but sin that dwelleth in me.
18   For I know that in me (that is, in my flesh,) dwelleth no good thing: for to will is present with me; but how to perform that which is good I find not.
19   For the good that I would I do not: but the evil which I would not, that I do.
20   Now if I do that I would not, it is no more I that do it, but sin that dwelleth in me.
21   I find then a law, that, when I would do good, evil is present with me.
22   For I delight in the law of God after the inward man:
23   But I see another law in my members, warring against the law of my mind, and bringing me into captivity to the law of sin which is in my members.
24   O wretched man that I am! Who shall deliver me from the body of this death?
25   I thank God through Jesus Christ our Lord. So then with the mind I myself serve the law of God; but with the flesh the law of sin.

Colossians 1:20
20   And, having made peace through the blood of his cross, by him to reconcile all things unto himself; by him, I say, whether they be things in earth, or things in heaven.

So here we are at Romans 8:1-4. The cross has made us free from sin and death. So, let's follow Jesus.

Romans 8:1-4
1   There is therefore now no condemnation to them which are in Christ Jesus, who walk not after the flesh, but after the Spirit.
2   For the law of the Spirit of life in Christ Jesus hath made me free from the law of sin and death.
3   For what the law could not do, in that it was weak through the flesh, God sending his own Son in the likeness of sinful flesh, and for sin, condemned sin in the flesh:
4   That the righteousness of the law might be fulfilled in us, who walk not after the flesh, but after the Spirit.

Discipleship Step #4: Follow Me

The fourth step of discipleship is an ongoing, continuous step. The fourth step is to follow Jesus every step of the way. After steps 1-3, we work to get our life in order. With God and Jesus Christ, we too can do like Jesus did, and start making disciples.

Matthew 4:18-19
18   And Jesus, walking by the sea of Galilee, saw two brethren, Simon called Peter, and Andrew his brother, casting a net into the sea: for they were fishers.
19   And he saith unto them, Follow me, and I will make you fishers of men.

Now that we are disciples, how do we get others into this discipleship? How do we get others to follow Jesus Christ, too?

Yes, preaching the gospel is one key way to get them to hear the word of God. Teaching the gospel is another key way for getting Christians to understand and learn more about Jesus Christ.

These keys, preaching and teaching, are used in mass communications to many people at once, but unlike God, it is not a one-on-one experience.

When boarding a ship or boat, passengers get on one at a time. Everyone who decides to be a disciple of Jesus Christ must follow these same steps. The four steps help you build a relationship with God and help you become a disciple. Only each of you individually can make these steps. You cannot become a disciple as a group!

Leaving all to follow Jesus does not stop once you become a disciple. Following Jesus is continuous. Jesus had twelve men who were his disciples. Remember step three. A disciple no longer walks after the flesh but after the Spirit.

In Acts 1: 4-8, Jesus leaves some instructions for his 11 disciples. These instructions are for us, too.

Acts 1:4-8

4   And, being assembled together with them, but wait for the promise of the Father, which, saith he, ye have heard of me.
5   for John truly baptized with water; but ye shall be baptized with the Holy Ghost not many days hence.
6   When they therefore were come together, they asked of him, saying, Lord, wilt thou at this time restore again the kingdom of Israel?

7   And he said unto them, It is not for me to know the times of the seasons, which the Father hath put in his own power.
8   But ye shall receive power, after that the Holy Ghost is come upon you: and ye shall be witnesses unto me both in Jerusalem, and in all Judaea, and in Samaria, and unto the uttermost part of the earth.

Verse 8 gives instruction about power. The power or presence of the Holy Spirit is a given in a true disciple of Christ.
Jesus also taught his disciples. The scripture says to study to show yourself approval, a workman rightly dividing the word of God.

Timothy 2:15
15   Study to show thyself approved unto God, a workman that needeth not to be ashamed, rightly dividing the word of truth.

The new disciple needs to embrace the power and the word of God in his or her personal life before he or she disciples others. Before you start an outreach/soul winning program, make sure that you yourself have completed and continually following ALL four of the steps Jesus has laid out in Matthew 16:24 and are studying the Word of God.

Matthew 16:24
24   Then said Jesus to his disciples, if any man will come after me, let him deny himself, ad take up his cross, and follow me.

Remember **Lights Out at Midnight** is for both the teacher and the disciple.

4. Love

Love Note #1: God is Love

Stop for a moment and ask yourself what love means to you. I thought about all the Greek terms for love; but then I decided to ask God. The first thing God said was, "God is Love."

I John 4:8

8   He that loveth not knoweth not God; for God is love.

The Scripture says, "God is love." Therefore, Love is God.

Love Note #2: Fruit of the Spirit

What is the fruit of the Spirit? What spirit are we talking about? Yes, that's right. We are talking about the Holy Spirit, or God's Spirit, which is one of the aspect of the God-heads in 3 persons:

- God the Father
- God the Son
- God the Holy Spirit

Therefore, all three persons make up the Fruit of God, the Spirit of God, in character for our lives and help guide how we should live.

Because the three God-heads are all one, this why it is called the fruit of the spirit and <u>not</u> the fruit<u>s</u> of the spirit<u>s</u>. I like to use the grape bunch as a symbol to explain the three God-heads as one. It is one fruit which many aspects.

It is important to recall that there are many bible interpretations: KJV, CEB, NIV, AMP and the list goes on.

I learned that there is importance in the order of things. For example, goodness is sixth and represents the stem of the grapes.

Love Note #3: Love in the First Place

What are the aspects that make up the fruit of the spirit? For me, Love, which is in the first place.

Love has many natural forms:
1. Love of God.
2. Love for my spouse.
3. Love of family, including children, parents, grandparents, aunts, uncles, and cousins. Family make up varies depending on your family. Especially in Tennessee, you can go up to fifth cousins!
4. Love of friends and Christian family.
5. Love of enemies.
6. Love of country, government, and police.

The list can go on and on when we talk about who we love, how we feel about love, and what we know about love.

Let's stop a moment and look at Love in Action, it's more than natural feeling!

We go back to our original statement in I John 4:8, we remember that "…God is love." Love becomes an action verb. Of course, we know God and some of us feel His presence, but Love requires actions. God is Love in action! God puts His love into actions in John 3:16.

John 3:16
16   For God so loved the world, that he gave his only begotten Son, that whosoever believeth in him should not perish, but have everlasting life.

God <u>so loved</u> the world, and gave His only Son. Love in action did not stop there. God, the Father, as the first God-head, puts love into action himself.

Luke 1:26-31
26   And in the sixth month the angel Gabriel was sent from God unto a city of Galilee, named Nazareth.
27   To a virgin espoused to a man whose name was Joseph, of the house of David; and the virgin's name was Mary.
28   And the angel came in unto her, and said, Hail, thou that art highly favoured, the Lord is with thee: blessed art thou among women.
29   And when she saw him, she was troubled at his saying, and cast in her mind what manner of salutation this should be.
30   And the angel said unto her, Fear not, Mary: for thou hast found favour with God.
31   And, behold, thou shalt conceive in thy womb, and bring forth a son, and shalt call his name Jesus.

Jesus, the second God-head, puts God's Love into action, too.

Mark 14:36
36   And he said, Abba, Father, all things are possible unto thee; take away this cup from me: nevertheless not what I will, but what thou wilt.

Jesus died, rose again, and is giving intercession on our behalf, sitting at the right of God the Father.

Love in action starts with God but doesn't end with the work of the son. It continues with the Love of the Holy Spirit, or the third person of the God-head.

Acts 1:7-8 & 2:1-4a
7 And he said unto them, It is not for you to know the times or the seasons, which the Father hath but into his own power.
8 But ye shall receive power, after that the Holy Ghost is come upon you: and ye shall be witnesses unto me both in Jerusalem, and in all Judaea, and in Samaria, and unto the uttermost part of the earth.
1 And when the day of Pentecost was fully come, they were all with one accord in one place.
2 And suddenly there came a sound from heaven as of a rushing mighty wind, and it filled all the house where they were sitting.
3 And there appeared unto them cloven tongues like as of fire, and it sat upon each of them.
4 And they were all filled with the Holy Ghost.

The Holy Spirit, or Holy Ghost, comes into action in the form of a teacher and instructor to show us the power of Love in action in our own lives.

The key to Love and most important teachable lesson can be found in I John 2:1-6, the key that opens the door. The greatest aspects of the Fruit of the Spirit can be found in verse 3 and 5.

1 John 2:1-6
1 My little children, these things write I unto you, that ye sin not. And if any man sin, we have an advocate with the Father, Jesus Christ the righteous:

2   And he is the propitiation for our sins: and not for ours only, but also for the sins of the whole world.

3   And hereby we do know that we know him, and we keep his commandments.

4   He that saith, I know him, and keepeth not his commandments, is a liar, and the truth is not in him.

5   But whoso keepeth his word, in him verily is the love of God perfected: hereby know we that we are in him.

6   He that saith he abideth in him ought himself also so to walk, even as he walked.

Look at the ending of verse 6b: "...so to walk, even as he walked." The word "so" relates back to God in John 3:16. God "...so loved..." the world. Then, the last phrase of 6b: "even as he walked." Who is he? Yes, Jesus Christ. The circling of the three God-heads in action.

Let's go back to verse 6. There is something of great importance there – isn't it? I went to the Common English Bible (CEB) version to make it simple.

1 John 2:6 (CEB) says, "The one who claims to remain in him (Jesus) ought to live in the same way as he (Jesus) lived."

The song "Love Lifted Me" by Ashmont Hill says: "Your love lifted me. / I am free to sing of your love, / Hallelujah, It's your love, It's your love, Yeah! / It's higher, higher, higher than heaven / It's deeper, deeper, deeper than oceans / It's greater, greater, greater than mountains.

Now, there is a part we all can play if we want everlasting life by living love in action. The love of the Father God was delivered by the love of the Son Christ Jesus. It was kept by the teaching and the power of the Holy Spirit, all working in action in and through us as the Fruit of the Spirit!

9. Self-Control (Temperance)

8. Gentleness (Meekness)

7. Faithfulness (Faith)

6. Goodness

5. Kindness (Mercy)

4. Patience (Longsuffering)

3. Peace

2. Joy

1. Love

Without the first aspect of the Fruit of the Spirit, God in us—Love in us—there would not be any other aspect of the fruit, for God is Love and God so loved us.

John 13:34-35
34 A new commandment I give unto you, That ye love one another; as I have loved you, that ye also love one another.
35 By this shall all men know that ye are my disciples, if ye have love to another.

GOD IN ACTION = LOVE ONE TO ANOTHER

ONE GOD

ONE LORD

ONE SPIRIT

ONE FRUIT

EAT IT ALL

Amen!!!

Part III:
Any Word from God?

Is There Any Word from the Lord?

God brought creation into existence, through His Word. He also destroyed the same world through the Flood and acts of judgment. Yet, God keeps his commitments and promises His Blessings.

Genesis 15:1
1   After these things the word of the Lord came unto Abram in a vision, saying, Fear not, Abram: I am thy shield, and thy exceeding great reward.

Sermon Outline

Is there any word?

Jeremiah 37:17
17   Then Zedekiah the king sent, and took him out: and the king asked him secretly in his house, and said, Is there any word from the Lord? And Jeremiah said, There is: for, said he, thou shalt be delivered into the hand of the king of Babylon.

Revelation 3:14-22
14   And unto the angel of the church of the Laodiceans write; These things saith the Amen, the faithful and true witness, the beginning of the creation of God;
15   I know thy works, that thou art neither cold nor hot: I would thou wert cold or hot.
16   So then because thou art luke-warm, and neither cold nor hot, I will spue thee out of my mouth.
17   Because thou sayest, I am rich, and increased with goods, and have need of nothing; and knowest not that thou art wretched, and miserable, and poor, and blind, and naked:
18   I counsel thee to buy of me gold tried in the fire, that thou mayest be rich; and white raiment, that thou mayest be clothed, and that the shame of thy nakedness do not appear; and anoint thine eyes with eyesalve, that thou mayest see.
19   As many as I love, I rebuke and chasten: be zealous therefore, and repent.
20   Behold, I stand at the door, and knock: if any man hear my voice, and open the door, I will come in to him, and will sup with him, and he with me.
21   To him that overcometh will I grant to sit with me in my throne, even as I also overcame, and am set down with my Father in his throne.

22   He that hath an ear, let him hear what the Spirit saith unto the churches.

Luke 15:18 (see below): "I will arise and go to my father..." Is there any word from the Lord? Yes, arise and go home. It's Homecoming Day.

Luke 15:11-19
11   And he said, A certain man had two sons:
12   And the younger of them said to his father, Father, give me the portion of goods that falleth to me. And he divided unto them his living.
13   And not many days after the younger son gathered all together, and took his journey into a far country, and there wasted his substance with riotous living.
14   And when he had spent all, there arose a mighty famine in that land; and he began to be in want.
15   And he went and joined himself to a citizen of that country; and he sent him into his fields to feed swine.
16   And he would fain have filled his belly with the husks that the swine did eat: and no man gave unto him.
17   And when he came to himself, he said, How many hired servants of my father's have bread enough to spare, and I perish with hunger!
18   I will arise and go to my father, and will say unto him, Father, I have sinned against heaven, and before thee.
19   And am no more worthy to be called thy son: make me as one of thy hired servants.

Yes, there are many words from the Lord.

John 3:16
16   For God so loved the world, that he gave his only begotten Son, that whosoever believeth in him should not perish, but have everlasting life.

Let not your heart be troubled. This passage goes on to say that there are many mansions in my Father's House. Where I am, may you be there also.

John 14: 1-4
1   Let not your heart be troubled: ye believe in God, believe also in me.
2   In my Father's house are many mansions: if it were not so, I would have told you. I go to prepare a place for you.
3   And if I go and prepare a place for you, I will come again, and receive you unto myself; that where I am, there ye may be also.
4   And whither I go ye know, and the way ye know.

Look at verse 6: Is there a Word from the Lord? In this verse, the Lord gives us direction to the Father's house.

John 14:6
6   Jesus saith unto him, I am the way, the truth, and the life: no man cometh unto the Father, but by me.

So, what is the problem that we continue to seek a word from the Lord?

Revelation 3:15
15   I know thy words, that thou art neither cold nor hot: I would thou wert cold or hot.

"I (the Lord) know thy (our) works:
1. not cold nor hot = lukewarm
2. rich – think we are or should be
3. increased with goods – all kinds of things, games, toys for the house, our children and for ourselves.
4. have need of nothing – if we don't have it, someone else will have it and will give it to us (example: government, friends, family), because everyone owes us.
5. Knowest not that – we are our biggest problem:
- wretched/pitiful/mean
- miserable
- poor
- blind
-naked

In all this mess, ask yourself: Is there a word from the Lord?

The answer is always, "Yes."

Revelation 3:20
20   Behold, I stand at the door, and knock: if any man hear my voice, open the door, I will come in to him, and will sup with him, and he with me.

Behold! Listen up! It is Homecoming Time. "I stand at the door and knock." My Lord wants a word with me, <u>if</u> I will listen.

Revelation 3:21-22
21   To him that overcometh will I grant to sit with me in my throne, even as I also overcame, and am set down with my Father in his throne.
22   He that hath an ear, let him hear what the Spirit saith unto the churches.

Yes, my Brothers and Sisters! There is a word from the Lord. Welcome Home!

What Is God Saying to You?

We may confuse the happenings around us with God speaking to us. How do we tell the difference?

Jeremiah is a character in the Old Testament. His name means "I have been established or exalted by God." The Book of Jeremiah tells of a chosen man who was supposed to help the Israelites turn away from false worship. He was motivated by the Word of God in times of trouble.

Jeremiah can be an important reminder for us. Hold onto the Word of God. Knowing the Word of God will help you tell the difference between what you experience in your life and how God is guiding you.

God's Word is a declaration of His commitment and His blessings.

Sermon Outline

Jeremiah 1:4
4   Then the word of the Lord came unto me, saying,

God spoke to Jeremiah in verse 11. "What seeth thou?"

Jeremiah 1:11
11   Moreover the word of the Lord came unto me, saying, Jeremiah, what seest thou? And I said, I see a rod of an almond tree.

Yes, we see all of these things going on in the world.

- Murder in Arizona, Colorado, St. Louis, New York, South Carolina
- Storms in New Orleans and Haiti
- Hurricanes in Texas, Florida, and Puerto Rico
- Fires in California
- Crime, drug use, and alcoholism
- Snow storms in unusual places
- Everyone coming out of the closet
- Churches having a zeal for God but not according to knowledge
- Church members being killed in their churches
- Being gunned down at concerts
- Trouble on every hand

But what do you see in the church world? So, what is God saying to us?

John 3:16
16   For God so loved the world, that he gave his only begotten Son, that whosoever believeth in him should not perish, but have everlasting life.

God Knows My Name

Sometimes God is described as a Shepherd. A shepherd's job is to make sure that his or her flock remains save and together. If one of the sheep becomes lost, the shepherd will go to great lengths to find the missing one.

Sometimes, you might be feeling like you are lost in the woods, alone, and that God has turned His back on you. But God is persistent in His search for the lost. God seeks you out, forgives you, and welcomes you back. Every time.

Amazing Grace!

How Sweet the Sound.

That saved a wretch like me!

I once was lost, but now am found;

Was blind, but now I see.

Sermon Outline

"I am not forgotten. The Lord knows my name." –Israel Haughton

Have you ever had a pity party with no one invited but you? Well, I have.

My pity party happened the day of the Church Business Meeting. Everyone remembers their first business meeting—things are not like Sunday morning service, where love is everywhere. No one knows who you are and don't want to hear what you have to say. O' God, does anyone know my name?

God spoke to me and He knows my name. The devil can take you down and out through sinful line. He can also take you up and out through self-pity, self-righteousness, or just being lost in the House like the brother in Luke 15:27-32.

Luke 15:27-32
27   And he said unto him, Thy brother is come; and thy father hath killed the fatted calf, because he hath received him safe and sound.
28   And he was angry, and would not go in: therefore came his father out, and entreated him.
29   And he answering said to his father, Lo, these many years do I serve thee, neither transgressed I at any time thy commandment: and yet thou never gavest me a kid, that I might make merry with my friends:
30   But as soon as this thy son was come, which hath devoured thy living with harlots, thou hast killed for him the fatted calf.
31   And he said unto him, Son, thou art ever with me, and all that I have in thine.

32   It was meet that we should make merry, and be glad: for this thy brother was dead, and is alive again; and was lost, and is found.

Brotherly love did not want to be heard, and you were in that deliverance state of being lost in the house. But God. Yes, He knows my name.

John 10:1-11;14
1   Verily, verily, I say unto you, He that entereth not by the door into the sheepfold, but climbeth up some other way, the same is a thief and a robber.
2   But he that entereth in by the door is the shepherd of the sheep.
3   To him the porter openeth; and the sheep hear his voice: and he calleth his own sheep by name, and leadeth them out.
4   And when he putteth forth his own sheep, he goeth before them, and the sheep follow him: for they know his voice.
5   And a stranger will they not follow, but will flee from him: for they know not the voice of strangers.
6   This parable spake Jesus unto them: but they understood not what things they were which he spake unto them.
7   Then said Jesus unto them again, Verily, verily, I say unto you, I am the door of the sheep.
8   All that ever came before me are thieves and robbers: but the sheep did not hear them.
9   I am the door: by me if any man enter in, he shall be saved, and shall go in and out, and find pasture.
10   The thief cometh not, but for to steal, and to kill, and to destroy: I am come that they might have life, and that they might have it more abundantly.
11   I am the good shepherd: the good shepherd giveth his life for the sheep.

14   I am the good shepherd, and know my sheep, and am known of mine.

Look at yourself. Does God/Christ Jesus know your name?

1 Corinthians 8:3
3   But if any man love God, the same is known of him.

God Changes Not!

God is the Creator and Sustainer of the universe. He has provided humankind with revelations about Himself through the natural world and through his Son, Jesus Christ.

God may be described with many adjectives. There might also be many analogies and images that remind us about God. These attributes and examples help us learn about God.

What we see, though, is that God doesn't change, even though the world around us does. If we hold onto God's Word, our faith will remain steady.

Sermon Outline

The Lord does not change.

Malachi 3:6
6   *For I am the Lord, I change not; therefore ye sons of Jacob are not consumed.*

Jesus Christ is the same yesterday, today, and always.

Hebrews 13:8
8   *Jesus Christ the same yesterday, and to day, and for ever.*

James 1:17
17   *Every good gift and every perfect gift is from above, and cometh down from the Father of lights, with whom is no variableness, neither shadow of turning.*

The counsel of the Lord stands forever. All generations may know his heart. We all know and agree that God is eternal and forever. He Is.

Psalm 33:11
11   *The counsel of the Lord standeth for ever, the thoughts of his heart to all generations.*

But times are changing. The Word that the founding fathers of most Christian organizations taught has not changed, because as Malachi 3 says, "God changes not." Even though times have changed from horse and buggy to Model T Ford to my 1995 Saturn, now, cars can run on electric power.

But, God Changes Not!

Think about all the things that have changed in your lifetime.
- From no wigs to wigs.
- From long sleeves to only short.
- From letter writing to phone calls. And now from texting to Facetime.
- From landlines to cell phones.
- From neighborhood churches to mega churches.
- From paper Bibles to computer Bibles.

We don't sing and preach like the old people – they were on fire. But what has changed?

God Changes Not!

Times have changed, things have changed, and yes, you have changed.
Maybe you left an unchanging God in the past because you changed. Remember, Hebrews 13:8. Jesus Christ is the same yesterday (during the founders' time). Jesus Christ is the same today (during your time). And Jesus Christ is the same forever (in the future, during the young people's time). Because:
- yesterday – is them.
- Today – is us.
- Forever – is the future until eternity.

Times change. And life changes.

But, God Changes Not!

I cannot live in yesterday, because yesterday is gone, yes, baby all gone.

I live today—God is today, God! So, I need to live God's word today—Sin not! Today, preach God's Word. In a changing world, I must let the world know that God does not change.

- Preaching is to save.
- Teaching is to keep them saved in a changing world.
- The promises of God never change.

Heaven or Hell? Do whatever it takes to tell the sinners the truth about God's Word.

- For God so loved you.
- Jesus died for you.
- Jesus rose for you.
- You <u>must</u> know God's voice.
- You <u>must</u> stop practicing sin.
- You <u>must</u> know God's Word.
- Your life/your walk <u>must</u> be in line with the unchanging God.
- God knows your name.

So, if you are a "Down at Cross" person, a "James Cleveland" person, a "No Cross, No Crown" person, an "Israel – I am Not Forgotten" person, or a T Bone Christian rapper lover, yes, your time zone might have changed, but remember, **God changes not!**

Sin is not a part of God's Kingdom.

1 John 3:1-10
1   Behold, what manner of love the Father hath bestowed upon us, that we should be called the sons of God: therefore the world knoweth us not, because it knew him not.
2   Beloved, now are we the sons of God, and it doth not yet appear what we shall be: but what know that, when he shall appear, we shall be like him; for we shall see him as he is.
3   And every man that hath this hope in him purifieth himself, even as he is pure.
4   Whosoever committeth sin transgresseth also the law: for sin is the transgression of the law.
5   And ye know that he was manifested to take away our sins; and in him is no sin.
6   Whosoever abideth in him sineth not: whosoever sinneth hath not seen him, neither known him.
7   Little children, let no man deceive you: he that doeth righteousness is righteous, even as he is righteous.
8   He that committeth sin is of the devil; for the devil sinneth from the beginning. For this purpose the Son of God was manifested, that he might destroy the works of the devil.
9   Whosoever is born of God doth not commit sin; for his seed remaineth in him: and he cannot sin, because he is born of God.
10   In this the children of God are manifest, and the children of the devil: whosoever doeth not righteousness is not of God, neither he that loveth not his brother.

Part IV:
Jesus & Me
Sermons from 2014-2015

For unto Us a Child Is Born

The birth of Jesus is our beginning. Only through Jesus Christ may you know God. He is your way, your light, and your truth. There wouldn't be Christianity without the birth of Jesus Christ.

Not only does he show you that life is eternal, but also he allows you to have a personal relationship with God. He shows us the way.

There are many names for Jesus in the bible, such as Alpha and Omega, Shepherd, Lamb of God, Prophet, Savior, Son of Man, and so on, but they all point to the Son of God.

From meager beginnings, he ascended to greatness. The news of his birth spread far and wide. Wise men came to bestow their blessings and gifts upon him. A reminder to all, that no matter your beginnings, greatest is born!

Sermon Outline

Wonderful, isn't He wonderful?

Isaiah 9:6
6   For us a child is born, unto us a son is given: and the government shall be upon his shoulder: and his name shall be called Wonderful, Counsellor, The mighty God, The everlasting Father, the Prince of Peace.

We use this scripture a lot but we do not understand what was going on at the time.
   1. Wickedness of Israel
   2. Pride
   3. Hypocrisy – pretense of having virtue, moral principle or religious belief that one does not really possess
   4. Impenitent – not feeling regret about one's sin or sins.

And yet, God tells Isaiah. In the midst of all this wickedness, the few that are holding on remember my promises:
   1. A child is born.
   2. A son is given.
   3. The government is on his shoulders.
   4. Call him Wonderful.

Saints, isn't He wonderful? Let me remind you!

1. For unto us a child is born.

Praise God, a child is born. A son is given. They shall call His name Jesus.

Luke 1:30-31
30   And the angel said unto her, Fear not, Mary: for thou hast found favour with God.
31   And, behold, thou shalt conceive in thy womb, and bring forth a son, and shalt call his name Jesus.

A great announcement to a virgin and then to a future husband. God's child is coming. It's tax time. Got to go to Bethlehem.
No room for them in the inn.

Luke 2:7
7   And she brought forth her first-born son, and wrapped him in swaddling clothes, and laid him in a manger; because there was no room for them in the inn.

2. Unto us a son is given.

John 3:16
16   For God so loved the world, that he gave his only begotten Son, that whosoever believeth in him should not perish, but have everlasting life.

The conditions of salvation are why the son was needed. The plan is set in place. The child grew.

Luke 2:40
40   And the child grew, and waxed strong in spirit, filled with wisdom: and the grace of God was upon him.

The son must be about his Father's business.

Luke 2:49
49   And he said unto him, How is it that ye sought me? wist ye not that I must be about my Father's business?

3. The government shall be upon His shoulders.

Matthew 3:17
17   And lo a voice from heaven, saying, This is my beloved Son, in whom I am well pleased.

Matthew 17:5
5   While he yet spake, behold, a bright cloud overshadowed them: and behold a voice out of the cloud, which said, This is my beloved Son, in whom I am well pleased; hear ye him.

Daniel 7:13-14
13   I saw in the night visions, and, behold, one like the Son of man came with the clouds of heaven, and came to the Ancient of days, and they brought him near before him.
14   And there was given him dominion, and glory, and a kingdom, that all people, nations, and languages, should serve him: his dominion is an everlasting dominion, which shall not be destroyed.

King of the Jews.

Matthew 2:2
2   Saying, Where is he that is born King of the Jews? For we have seen his star in the east, and are come to worship him.

Heard the king was jealous and troubled as well as all of Jerusalem.

Matthew 2:6
6   And thou Bethlehem, in the land of Juda, art not the least among the princes of Juda: for our of thee shall come a Governor, that shall rule my people Israel.

Governor, that shall rule my people Israel.

Matthew 2:12
12   And being warned of God in a dream that they should not return to Herod, they departed into their own country another way.

4. And He shall be called Wonderful.

Call him:
>Wonderful
>Counselor
>The Mighty God
>The Everlasting Father
>Prince of Peace

Song: "Isn't He wonderful? To me He so wonderful to know that Jesus is mine."
He was called wonderful before he was born.

Isaiah 9:6
6   For us a child is born, unto us a son is given: and the government shall be upon his shoulder: and his name shall be called Wonderful, Counsellor, The mighty God, The everlasting Father, the Prince of Peace.

New Testament saints who call him wonderful:

Simeon and Ana could not die until they saw Jesus

Luke 3:25-38

John the Baptist, the forerunner.

John 1:26,29
26   John answered them, saying, I baptize with water: but there standeth one among you whom ye know not;
29   The next day John seeth Jesus coming unto him, and saith, Behold the Lamb of God, which taketh away the sin of the world.

Have you seen Him?

John 14:8-10;17
8   Philip saith unto him, Lord, show us the Father, and it sufficeth us.
9   Jesus saith unto him, Have I been so long time with you, and yet hast thou not known me, Philip? He that hath seen me hath seen the Father; and how sayeth thou then, Show us the Father?
10   Believest thou not that I am in the Father, and the Father is in me? the words that I speak unto you I speak not of myself: but the Father that dwelleth in me, he doeth the works.
17   Even the Spirit of truth; whom the world cannot receive, because it seeth him not, neither knoweth hin: but ye know him; for he dwelleth with you, and shall be in you.

Do you want to see Him? What is your wish for your soul? And how do you plan to get it? All souls want to go to heaven, but all flesh wants to do it their way. The problem is getting along with the plan.

John 14:1-6
1   Let not your heart be troubled: ye believe in God, believe also in me.
2   In my Father's house are many mansions: if it were not so, I would have told you. I go to prepare a place for you.
3   And if I go and prepare a place for you, I will come again, and receive you unto myself: that where I am, there ye may be also.
4   And whither I go ye know, and the way ye know.s
5   Thomas saith unto him, Lord, we know not whither thou goest; and how can we know the way?
6   Jesus saith unto him, I am the way, the truth, and the life: no man cometh unto the Father, but by me.

Song: "To me, He is so wonderful. To me, he is so wonderful to know that Jesus is mine."

Can Anything Good Come Out of Nazareth?

Nathanael was introduced to Jesus by his friend, Philip. Nathanael, originally from Galilee, knew of Nazareth as a small town. He also knew that Jesus grew up there, but because the size of the town, he was unconvinced that Jesus could be what Philip said—the redeemer of Israel.

In the Book of John, Nathanael and Philip are having a conversation. Nathanael is asking Philip, "Can anything good come out of Nazareth?" Philip doesn't try to explain, he simply says, "Come and see."

In your life, you might find yourself asking, "Is Jesus a big deal?" Answer your own question with, "Come and see!"

Sermon Outline

Beginning Song: Jesus, you are the center of my joy!

Ending Song: O' How He Loves You and Me

Subject: Can Anything Good Come Out of Nazareth?

John 1:45-46
45   Philip findeth Nathanael, and saith unto him, We have found him, We have found him, of whom Moses in the law, and the prophets, did write, Jesus of Nazarreth, the son of Joseph.
46   And Nathanael said undo him, Can there any good thing come out of Nazareth? Philip saith unto him, Come and see.

Nazareth was a small town in Galilee. Jesus is from Nazareth, and he is the son of Joseph. His story did not just start there.

Genesis 3:15
15   And I will put my enmity between thee and the woman, and between thy seen and her seed; it shall bruise thy head, and thou shalt bruise his heel.

In the beginning, her seed is Jesus, the promised seed.

Genesis 12:3
3   And I will bless them that bless thee, and curse him that curseth thee: and in thee shall all families of the earth be blessed.

God promises to Abram a promised seed. All families on the earth will be blessed.

Number 20:8
8   Take the rod, and gather thou the assembly together, thou, and Aaron thy brother, and speak ye unto the rock before their eyes; and it shall give forth his water, and thou shalt bring forth to them water out of the rock: so thou shalt give the congregation and their beasts drink.

The Lord spoke to Moses and told him to speak to the rock (that rock was Jesus). Inside the rock, there is water in a dry land.

O' yes, Jesus was born in Bethlehem!

1 Samuel 16:1
16   And the Lord said unto Samuel, How long wilt thou mourn for Saul, seeing I have rejected him from reigning over Israel? fill thine horn with oil, and go, I will send thee to Jesse the Bethlehemite: for I have provided me a king among his sons.

The Spirit of the Lord came upon David.

1 Samuel 16:12-13
12   And he sent, and brought him in. Now he was ruddy, and withal of a beautiful countenance, and goodly to look to. And the Lord said, Arise, anoint him: for this is he.
13   Then Samuel took the horn of oil, and anointed him in the midst of his brethren: and the spirit of the Lord came upon David from that day forward. So Samuel rose up, and went to Ramah.

The man's seed is Jesus.

Acts 13:22-23
22   And when he had removed him, he raised up unto them David to be their king: so whom also he gave testimony, and said, I have found David the son of Jesse, a man after mine own heart, which shall fulfil all my will.
23   Of this man's seed hath God according to his promise raised unto Israel a Saviour, Jesus:

Isaiah 11:1-5
1 And there shall come forth a rod out of the stem of Jesse, and a Branch shall grow out of his roots:
2   And the spirit of the Lord shall rest upon him, the spirit of wisdom and understanding, the spirit of counsel and might, the spirit of knowledge and of the fear of the Lord;
3   And shall make him of quick understanding in the fear of the Lord: and he shall not judge after the sight of his eyes, neither reprove after the hearing of his ears:
4   But with righteousness shall he judge the poor, and reprove with equity for the meek of the earth: and he shall smite the earth with the rod of his mouth, and with the breath of his lips shall he slay the wicked.
5   And righteousness shall be the girdle of his loins, and faithfulness the girdle of his reins.

Yes, Jesse's seed. The Spirit of the Lord shall rest upon him the Spirit of wisdom and understanding, the Spirit of counsel and might, the Spirit of knowledge, and of the fear of the Lord. Look at baby Jesus. Can any good thing come out of Nazareth?

Isaiah 52:1
1   Awake, awake: put on thy strength, O Zion; put on my beautiful garments, O Jerusalem, the holy city: for henceforth there shall no more come into thee the uncircumcised and the unclean.

Awake, awake, put on thy strength, O Zion!

Isaiah 53:1
1   Who hath believed our report? And to whom is the arm of the Lord revealed?

Remember, can anything good come from Nazareth?

Isaiah 53:2-5
2   For he shall grow up before him as a tender plant, and as a root out of a dry ground: he hath no form nor comeliness; and when we shall see him, there is no beauty that we should desire him.
3   He is despised and rejected of men; a man of sorrows, and acquainted with grief: and we hid as it were our faces from him; he was despised and we esteemed him not.
4   Surely he hath borne our griefs, and carried our sorrows: yet we did esteem him stricken, smitten of God, and afflicted.
5   But he was wounded for our transgressions, he was bruised for our iniquities: the chastisement of our peace was upon him; and with his stripes we are healed.

Jesus as a wheel, right in the middle of the wheel.

Ezekiel 10:10
10   And as for their appearances, they four had one likeness, as if a wheel had been in the midst of a wheel.

Daniel 3:23-25

23   And these three men, Shadrach, Meshach, and Abednego, fell down bound into the midst of the burning fiery furnace.

24   Then Nebuchadnezzar the king was astonished, and rose up in haste, and spake, and said unto his counselors, Did not we cast three men bound into the midst of the fire? They answered and said unto the king, True, O king.

25   He answered and said, Lo, I see four men loose, walking In the midst of the fire, and they have no hurt; and the form of the fourth is like the Son of God.

Happy Birthday, Jesus! Nebuchadnezzar saw the form of the forth man, who is like the Son of God.

Daniel 6:22

22   My God hath sent his angel, and hath shut the lions' mouths, that they have not hurt me: forasmuch as before him innocency was found in me; and also before thee, O king, have I done no hurt.

Daniel saw Jesus as the one who shut the lions' mouths. Can anything good come out of Nazareth? Jonah met Jesus in the belly of a great fish.

Jonah 2:1-10

1   Then Jonah prayed unto the Lord his God out of the fish's belly,

2   And I said, I cried by reason of mine affliction unto the Lord, and he heard me; out of the belly of hell cried I, and thou heardest my voice.

3   For thou hadst cast me into the deep, in the midst of the seas; and the floods compassed me about: all thy billows and thy waves passed over me.

4   Then I said, I am cast out of thy sight; yet I will look again toward thy holy temple.
5   The waters compassed me about, even to the soul: the depth closed me round about, the weeds were wrapped about my head.
6   I went down to the bottoms of the mountains; the earth with her bars was about me for ever: yet hast thou brought up my life from corruption, O Lord my God.
7   When my soul fainted within me I remembered the Lord: and my prayer came in unto thee, into thine holy temple.
8   They that observe lying vanities forsake their own mercy.
9   But I will sacrifice unto thee with the voice of thanksgiving; I will pay that that I have vowed. Salvation is of the Lord.
10   And the Lord spake unto the fish, and it vomited out Jonah upon the dry land.

Salvation is of the Lord. *[reread verse 9]*

Zechariah 3:8
8   Fear now, O Joshua the high priest, thou, and thy fellows that sit before thee: for they are men wondered at: for, behold, I will bring forth my servant the Branch.

Zechariah 6:12
12   And speak unto him, saying, Thus speaketh the Lord of hosts, saying, Behold the man whose name is The Branch; and he shall grow up out of his place, and he shall build the temple of the Lord:

Recall the branch. Jesse's branch, the seed of Abraham, Isaac, Jacob, and David. Jesus is the branch. Can anything good come out of Nazareth?

Malachi 1:2
*2	I have loved you, saith the Lord. Yet ye say, Wherein hast thou loved us? Was not Esau Jacob's brother? Saith the Lord: yet I loved Jacob,*

I have loved you. Yes, Jesus loves me. Happy Birthday Jesus! Yes, Jesus loves us.

Malachi 3:1
*1	Behold, I will send my messenger, and he shall prepare the way before me: and the Lord, whom ye seek, shall suddenly come to his temple, even the messenger of the covenant, whom ye delight in: behold, he shall come, saith the Lord of hosts.*

He sends his messenger to tell us to get ready. Yes, something good can come out of the Nazareth, after 400 years of silence and over 42 generations.
Hark the Herald Angel Sing. Glory to the newborn king. Emmanuel, God is with us.

Matthew 1:23
*23	Behold, a virgin shall be with child, and shall bring forth a son, and they shall call his name Emmanuel, which being interpreted is, God with us.*

Called His name Jesus.

Matthew 1:25
*25	And knew her not till she had brought forth her firstborn son: and he called his name Jesus.*

Yes, Nathaneal, Something Good can come out of Nazareth.

Happy Birthday, Jesus! Thank you for discipling me.

Song: "O' How He Love You and Me."

Must Jesus Bear the Cross?

Thomas Shepherd sings, "Must Jesus bear the cross alone, and all the world go free? No, there's a cross for everyone, and there's a cross for me."

When we think about the crucifixion of Jesus, we only think about how Jesus must bear the Cross for our sins, for the salvation of the world. We don't think about the cross that each of us must also bear.

When we think about Jesus and the cross, we also probably don't know about Simon of Cyrene and the cross that he had to bear, as he walked alongside Jesus to his death.

Simon of Cyrene was a visitor to Jerusalem. He was a devout follower of Jesus. The Book of Mark mentions him. He was selected by the Romans to help Jesus carry his cross.

When we think about Jesus and the cross, we probably don't think about our cross we must carry.

Sermon Outline

Must Jesus bear the cross alone, and all the world go free? That is an age-old song, but it is still a good question.

The answer comes back. No, there's a cross for everyone, and there's a cross for me.

Jesus makes the statement, "take up his cross, and follow me."

Matthew 16:24
24   Then said Jesus unto his disciples, If any man will come after me, let him deny himself, and take up his cross, and follow me.

There was a man named Simon, who was to carry Jesus' cross all the way to Golgatha.

Mark 15:21-22
21   And they compel one Simon a Cyrenian, who passed by, coming out of the country, the father of Alexander and Rufus, to bear his cross.
22   And they bring him unto the place Golgotha, which is, being interpreted, The place of a skull.

Not much is written about this man—Simon of Cyrene—but these three things we know:
1. He was a Cyrenaic.
2. He was a passerby.
3. He had two sons: Alexander and Rufus.

Some believe that he was a black man. I don't know, yet I believe these four feelings had to cross his mind:

1. Surprise
2. Annoyance
3. Reluctance
4. Embarrassment

Surprise.
Why did you, Roman soldier, pull me out of the crowded street? I am just passing by. I am a stranger in Jerusalem. I don't know what's going on. Who is this man? Why me?

As we bear our own cross, we may ask, "Why me?" You do all the right things. Why me?

Annoy.
What about my plans for today? Maybe his sons and he had plans that did not include cross bearing. Have you ever got annoyed when something or someone changes your plans?

I was once annoyed three or so days before my mission trip to Africa. I had my bags packed, ticket in my hand, and was ready to go. I woke up and could not walk. This was the last thing I wanted to happen at that time.

Reluctance.
There is a song from the 1960s called, "Please Mr. Custer, I don't want to go." Why should I have to do this for a stranger? This stranger could be a murderer for all I know. Reluctance is a game changer that screams, "I don't want to go!"

Mark 19:23-24
23   And they give him to drink wine mingled with myrrh: but he received it not.
24   And when they had crucified him, they parted his garments, casting lots upon them, what every man should take.

Embarrassment.

Simon must have been thinking, "What will my friends, sons, and all these people think about me?" Peer pressure causes us to do things we don't want to, or do things with embarrassment.

"What will people think?"

Young people don't care, as long as their friends are okay with it. That way, they don't get embarrassed.

As an adult, though, it's all about what others think about or how they react to what we're doing.

But, embarrassments weigh heavy on your subconscious mind.

As women over fifty, they don't care what you think…to some degree.

No, Simon, your feelings of **surprise**—shows us honor to be called out.

No, Simon, your feelings of **annoyance**—shows us that my plan to live for Christ annoys my old life.

No, Simon, your feelings of **reluctance**—shows us that at first I had to deny myself and pick up my own cross.

No, Simon, your feelings of **embarrassment**—shows us that this time Jesus is carrying both my cross and me.

No, Simon, you will always be remembered.

Must Jesus bear the cross alone?

Surprise: I am calling you out.

Annoy: The devil is always with annoyance. I must rely on Jesus.

Reluctance: I will think of many reasons why not to pick up your cross and follow Jesus.

Embarrassment: I will say, "Not now!" but remember, "No, there's a cross for everyone."

But in the end, if your name is not in the book of life. You must have let Jesus carry His own cross. No cross, no crown…pick up your cross and follow Jesus!

Must Jesus Bear the Cross Alone?
by Thomas Shepherd:

Must Jesus bear the cross alone,
And all the world go free?
No, there's a cross for everyone,
And there's a cross for me.

How happy are the saints above,
Who once were sorr'wing here!
But now they taste unmingled love,
And joy without a tear.

The consecrated cross I'll bear
Till death shall set me free;
And then go home my crown to wear,
For there's a crown for me.

Upon the crystal pavement down
At Jesus' pierced feet,
Joyful I'll cast my golden crown
And His dear Name repeat.

O precious cross! O glorious crown!
O resurrection day!
When Christ the Lord from heav'n comes down
And bears my soul away.

When I See Jesus—Amen!

No matter who we are or where we come from, Jesus is for us. Whether we are rich or poor, Jesus is for us.

Jesus teaches us how to show kindness for everyone, even if they aren't like us, or if they are less fortunate than we are.

Jesus' stories are parables that show his twelve disciples how to follow him. They also show us how to live a God-filled life.

Always look for the paradox. For example, "the last shall be first, and the first last." Many are called but few are chosen.

Blessed are the meek for they shall inherit the earth.

Sermon Outline

When I see Jesus—Amen! The rich man also died and was buried.

Luke 16:22
22   And it came to pass, that the beggar died, and was carried by the angels into Abraham's bosom: the rich man also died, and was buried;

The rich has no name. The beggar's name was Lazarus. Jesus had just spoken with the rich young ruler.

Mark 10:17-23
17   And when he was gone forth into the way, there came one running, and kneeled to him, Good master, what shall I do that I may inherit eternal life?
18   And Jesus said unto him, Why callest thou me good? There is none good but one, that is, God.
19   Thou knowest the commandments, Do not commit adultery, Do not kill, Do not steal, Do not bear false witness, Defraud not, Honour thy father and mother.
20   And he answered and said unto him, Master, all these have I observed form my youth.
21   Then Jesus beholding him loved him, and said unto him, One thing thou lackest: go thy way, sell whatsoever thou hast, and give to the poor, and thou shalt have treasure in heaven: and come, take up the cross, and follow me.
22   And he was sad at that saying, and went away grieved: for he had great possessions.

23   And Jesus looked round about, and saith unto his disciples, How hardly shall they that have riches enter into the kingdom of God!

Yes, the first shall be last and the last shall be first.

Matthew 19:30
30   But many that are first shall be last; and the last shall be first.

If you note the rich in Jesus' parable never had a name, but the beggar's name was Lazarus. A rich, young ruler asks, "What shall I do that I may inherit eternal life?"

Mark 10:17
17   And when he was gone forth into the way, there came one running, and kneeled to him, Good master, what shall I do that I may inherit eternal life?

When I see Jesus, I don't want to be last; neither did Peter, so he asked the question. "We have left everything to follow you."

Mark 10:28-30
28   Then peter began to say unto him, Lo, we have left all, and have followed thee.
29   And Jesus answered and said, Verily I say unto you, There is no man that hath left house, or brethren, or sisters, or father, or mother, or wife, or children, or lands, for my sake, and the gospel's,

30   But he shall receive an hundredfold now in this time, houses, and brethren, and sisters, and mothers, and children, and lands, with persecutions; and in the world to come eternal life.

Eternal life, Praise God. Eternal life. So when I see Jesus—Amen!

Amen, Amen, Let the words of my mouth and the meditation of my heart be acceptable to Jesus, because you are my Lord, my rock, and my redeemer. Amen!

Psalm 19:14
14   Let the words of my mouth, and the meditation of my heart, be acceptable in thy sight, O Lord, my strength, and my redeemer.

Like Abraham to the rich man, the rich man can be saved too.

Luke 16:31
31   And he said unto him, if they hear not Moses and the prophets, neither will they be persuaded, though one rose from the dead.

John 3:16 says, "*...whosoever...*" When I see Jesus—Amen!

What is Jesus Doing for Me?

Jesus works in each of our lives. His love affects us differently, but rest assured, he is working on our behalf. We are reminded to continue to glorify Jesus, even though He is no longer here in in the flesh. Christ shows up in each of our lives. We just have to look for his presence. Each of us is an heir of God through Christ.

Jesus will show you who you are. He will also show you who you aren't. On a daily basis, check in. Where does Jesus show up? How is he working in your life?

Sermon Outline

Write down the things that Jesus is doing for you. Keep them for yourself. Here are a few things that Jesus is doing for me.

The Giver of the Spirit.

1 John 4:1-6
1   Beloved, believe not every spirit, but try the spirits whether they are of God: because many false prophets are gone out into the world.
2   Hereby know ye the Spirit of God: Every spirit that confesseth that Jesus Christ is come in the flesh is of God:
3   And every spirit that confesseth not that Jesus Christ is come in the flesh is not of God: and this is that spirit of antichrist, whereof ye have heard that it should come; and even now already is it in the world.
4   Ye are of God, little children, and have overcome them: because greater is he that is in you, than he that is in the world.
5   They are of the world: therefore speak they of the world, and the world heareth them.
6   We are of God: he that knowth God heareth us; he that is not of God heareth not us. Hereby know we the spirit of truth, and the spirit of error.

John 16:13
13   Howbeit when he, the Spirit of truth, is come, he will guide you into all truth: for he shall not speak of himself; but whatsoever he shall hear, that shall he speak: and he will show you things to come.

Watcher of the Danger Zone.

Galatians 4:7-11
7   Wherefore thou art no more a servant, but a son; and if a son, then an heir of God through Christ.
8   Howbeit then, when ye knew not God, ye did service unto them which by nature are no gods.
9   But now, after that ye have known God, or rather are known of God, how turn ye again to the weak and beggarly elements, whereunto ye desure again to be in bondage?
10   Ye observe days, and months, and times, and years.
11   I am afraid of you, lest I have bestowed upon you labour in vain.

The Liberator.

Galatians 5:1
1   Stand fast therefore in the liberty wherewith Christ hath make us free, and be not entangled again with the yoke of bondage.

Tell me who I am.

1 Peter 2:9
9   But ye are a chosen generation, a royal priesthood, an holy nation, a peculiar people; that ye should show forth the praises of him who hath called you out of darkness into his marvelous light:

Tell me who I am not.

Ephesians 4:25-32
25   Wherefore putting away lying, speak every man truth with his neighbor: for we are members one of another.

26   Be ye angry, and sin not: let not the sun go down upon your wrath:
27   Neither give place to the devil.
28   Let him that stole steal no more: but rather let him labour, working with his hands the thing which is good, that he may have to give to him that needeth.
29   Let no corrupt communication proceed out of your mouth, but that which is good to the use of edifying, that it may minister grace unto the hearers.
30   And grieve not the holy Spirit of God, whereby ye are sealed unto the day of redemption.
31   Let all bitterness, and wrath, and anger, and clamour, and evil speaking, be put away from you, with all malice:
32   And be ye kind one to another, tenderhearted, forgiving one another, even as God for Christ's sake hath forgiven you.

Ephesians 5:3-7
3   But fornication, and all uncleanness, or covetousness, let it not be once named among you, as becometh saints;
4   Neither filthiness, nor foolishtalking, nor jesting, which are not convenient: but rather giving of thanks.
5   For this ye know, that no whore-monger, nor unclean person, nor covetous man, who is an idolater, hath any interitance in the kingdom of Christ and of God.
6   Let no man deceive you with vain words: for because of these things cometh the wrath of God upon the children of disobedience.
7   Be not ye therefore partakers with them.

Bishop of My Soul: My Keeper

John 17:11
11   And now, I am no more in the world, but these are in the world, and I come to thee. Holy Father, keep through thine

own name those whom thou hast given me, that they make be one, as we are.

John 17:15-17
15   I pray not that thou shouldest take them out of the world, but that thou shouldest keep them from evil.
16   They are not of the world, even as I am not of the world.
17   Sanctify them through thy through: thy word is truth.

Look at your answers about what Jesus is doing for you. Do yours come anywhere near to the sixth point of what Jesus is doing for me? Jesus is the Bishop of My Soul; he is my Keeper. Then you need to rethink or talk to Jesus and see what He is doing. And see if any one of your answers lines up with the Word of God.

Then, Hosanna. Hosanna blessed be the rock of my salvation!

Isaiah 52:1-6
1   Awake, awake: put on thy strength, O Zion; put on thy beautiful garments, O Jerusalem, the holy city: for henceforth there shall no more come into thee the uncircumcised and the unclean.
2   Shake thyself from the dust; arise, and sit down, O Jerusalem: loose thyself from the bands of thy neck, O captive daughter of Zion.
3   For thus saith the Lord, Ye have sold yourselves for naught; and ye shall be redeemed without money.
4   For thus saith the Lord God, My people went down aforetime into Egypt to sojourn there; and the Assyrian oppressed them without cause.
5   Now therefore, what have I here, saith the Lord, that my people is taken away for nought? They that rule over them make them to howl, saith the Lord; and my name continually everyday is blasphemed.

6   Therefore my people shall know my name: therefore they shall know in that day that I am he that doth speak: behold, it is I.

Part V:
Jesus & You
Sermons from 2014-2015

What Do You Want Jesus to Do?

There are several stories in the New Testament, which tell of Jesus descending into a multitude of people. There are many people around. You might imagine that everyone is talking, creating a level of noise.

Then, Jesus walks past beggars and individuals with problems. Not only do these individuals speak up, but they call out to him. In a large crowd of talkative individuals, it would be hard to hear one person's call. But Jesus hears the calls from these people. And he stops, and asks, "What do you want me to do?" So, the blind man says, "Yes, Jesus, I would like my sight back." And the man receives his sight.

If you can imagine yourself sitting in a large group of people. Then imagine that Jesus walks by. You call out to him, telling him about one of your most robust problems. Not only does he stop to hear you, but he also stops and asks, "What would you like me to do?" So, tell me, what would you like Jesus to do?

Sermon Outline

In the Book of Matthew, there is a story about two blind men.

Matthew 20:29-34
29   And as they departed from Jericho, a great multitude followed him.
30   And, behold, <u>two blind men</u> sitting by the way side, when they heard that Jesus passed by, cried out, saying, Have mercy on us, O Lord, thou son of David.
31   And the multitude rebuked them, because the should hold their peace: but they cried the more, saying, Have mercy on us, O Lord, thou son of David.
32   And Jesus stood still, and called them, and said, What will ye that I shall do unto you?
33   They say unto him, Lord, that our eyes may be opened.
34   So Jesus had compassion on them, and touched their eyes: and immediately their eyes received sight, and they followed him.

In the Book of Mark, the blind man is called by name, Bartimaeus.

Mark 10:46-52
46   And they came to Jericho, and as he went out of Jericho with his disciples and a great number of people, blind <u>Bartimaeus</u>, the son of Timaeus, sat by the highway side begging.
47   And when he heard that it was Jesus of Nazareth, he began to cry out, and say, Jesus, thou son of David, have mercy on me.

48   And many charged him that he should hold his peace: but he cried the more a great deal. Thou son of David have mercy on me.
49   And Jesus stood still, and commanded him to be called. And they call the blind man, saying unto him, Be of good comfort, rise; he calleth thee.
50   And he, casting away his garment, rose, and came to Jesus.
51   And Jesus answered and said unto him, What wilt thou that I should do unto thee? The blind man said unto him, Lord, that I might receive my sight.
52   And Jesus said unto him, Go thy way; thy faith hath made thee whole. And immediately he received his sight, and followed Jesus in the way.

In the Book of Luke, he is referred to as a blind beggar.

Luke 18:35-43
35   And it came to pass, that as he was come nigh unto Jerricho, <u>a certain blind man sat by the way side begging</u>:
36   And hearing the multitude pass by, he asked what it meant.
37 And they told him, that Jesus of Nazareth passeth by.
38   And he cried, saying, Jesus, thou son of David, have mercy on me.
39   And they which went before rebuked him, that he should hold his peace: but he cried so much the more. Thou son of David, have mercy on me.
40   And Jesus stood, and commanded him to be brought unto him: and when he was come near, he asked him.
41   Saying, What wilt thou that I shall do unto thee? And he said, Lord, that I may receive my sight.

42   And Jesus said unto him, Receive thy sight: thy faith hath saved thee.
43   And immediately he received his sight, and following him, florifying God: and all the people, when they saw it, gave praise unto God.

The point is that they were blind and this was their last opportunity; Jesus was passing by. And the question was and still is, "What will ye that I shall do unto you?" Today, Jesus is passing by—What do you want him to do?

It has been a long trip for Jesus from heaven to earth to glory and home again. And yet, Jesus heard a beggar cry among a multitude of voices. That small cry made Jesus stand still. Why would Jesus have stood still on this road back to glory and then home? Because John wrote about it.

John 3:16-18
16   For God so loved the world, that he gave his only begotten Son, that whosoever believeth in him should not perish, but have everlasting life.
17   For God sent not his Son into the world to condemn the world; but that the world through him might be saved.
18   He that believeth on him is not condemned: but he that believeth not is condemned already, because he hath not believed in the name of the only begotten Son of God.

Jesus is still working on His original call. Go—let them believe and be saved.

Yes, the trip is almost over. The triumphant entry into Jerusalem is about to start. Jesus is on the road to glory then home to sit on the right hand of God. Yet,

He still has time to hear a beggar cry. "Son of David have mercy on me."

Have you been blind enough? Have your sins and weight still have you down?

Does your soul want to cry, "Jesus—Son of David—have mercy on me."

Then, Just Cry Out!

Jesus is passing by. He is still listening to hear your cry.

The question is still the same, "What will thou that I shall do unto thee?" Jesus is standing still. Just come.

Yes they were rebuked. They cried out!

Jesus is standing and listening. Just ask Him!

Matthew 7:7
7   *Ask and it shall be given you; seek, and ye shall find; knock, and it shall be opened unto you:*

Ask—they received their sight.

Seek—look to Jesus. He is waiting.

Knock—open "what wash away my sins, nothing by the blood of Jesus." He can make you whole again.

That is what Jesus can do—Just come and give God the glory!

It's All About Jesus. It's Not About You!

When we live our lives, we might feel like we are just going through the motions. We may feel like all we are doing is checking our to-dos off the list. Whatever is on our "to-do list," we might feel like we just have to get things done. In the middle of getting things done, we may feel sad, depressed, troubled, or lost. Life might feel hard or hopeless.

We are reminded that God is our Great Comforter. The Book of John reminds us that the only way to get to God is through Jesus. Jesus will show us that we don't need to be troubled. He urges us to believe in Him. Rest assured that He believes in us.

Make space in your life for God. Make space in your life for Jesus. This will take patience, discipline, and obedience. But when we make space in our life for the divine, the divine makes space for us.

Jesus will show us which way to go. He will show us what really belongs on our "to-do list" and which way we must turn.

Whenever you doubt, remember that Jesus is the truth. Not only will He show you the way, He'll show you that He is the way. Not only will he give you your life, He'll show you that he is life.

Sermon Outline

In 2014, I heard Elder Charles William's sermon was entitled, **"Now is the Time."**

John 7:6
6   Then Jesus said unto them, My time is not yet come: but your time is alway ready.

It's all about Jesus. It's not about you. It's all about Jesus!

John 14:1-6
1   Let not your heart be troubled: ye believe in God, believe also in me.
2   In my Father's house are many mansions: if it were not so, I would have told you. I go to prepare a place for you.
3   And if I go and prepare a place for you, I will come again, and receive you unto myself: that where I am, there ye may be also.
4   And whither I go ye know, and the way ye know.
5   Thomas saith unto him, Lord, we know not whither thou goest; and how can we know the way?
6   Jesus saith unto him, I am the way, the truth, and the life: no man cometh unto the Father, but by me.

Get ready, get ready. It's a long, long, lonely journey. You're going to need King Jesus every step of the way.

Thomas is like us. He is like me. I really don't know the way. Truth be known. Believe in Jesus, read your Bible, go to church, live a good life, don't do this or that, and when we die, we will go to heaven.

Jesus tells us how in chapter 14, verse 6. He is the Way. He is the Truth. He is the Life.

It's a long, lonely journey. You are going to need King Jesus.

The first thing Jesus told us was to not be troubled.

Then, he told us to prepare a place. When we get ready, Jesus will come to us. He will show us which way to go.

Even when Thomas doubted the way to go, even when we doubt what's next, remember to get ready. Jesus will come to us. He will show us which way to go.

Remember, it's all about Jesus, not about you. It's all about Jesus, and it's a long journey, but go with Jesus every step of the way.

Has Jesus Chosen You to Be His Friend?

Many times, in the Bible, Jesus befriends disciples, servants, gentiles, and others. He even befriends and loves sinners, enemies, and those who killed him. He loved them, anyway!

Each of us must get closer to God through our relationship with Christ Jesus. Through the parables and stories of Jesus tell us how to establish a friendship with Jesus.

Imagine as if Jesus were your best friend. Best friends don't leave you when times are tough. In fact, they are there for you exactly when times are hard. Jesus will never leave you.

You trust best friends with your shame and darkest secrets. You can trust Jesus the same way.

Think of Jesus as your best friend, the one who loves you the most, because you are you. He loves you just the way you are.

Sermon Outline

John 15:12-17
12   This is my commandment, That ye love one another, as I have loved you.
13   Greater love hath no man than this, that a man lay down his life for his friends.
14   Ye are my friends, if ye do whatsoever I command you.
15   Henceforth I call you not servants; for the servant knoweth not what his lord doeth: but I have called you friends; for all things that I have heard of my Father I have made known unto you.
16   Ye have not chosen me, but I have chosen you, and ordained you, that ye should go and bring forth fruit, and that your fruit should remain: that whatsoever ye shall ask of the Father in my name, he may give it you.
17   These things I command you, that ye love one another.

Has Jesus chosen you to be His friend?
We must:
1. Love one another.
2. Be willing to lay down our life for our friend.
3. Do whatever Jesus commands us to do.
4. Serve each other. We are no more servants, but we must.
5. Be chosen and ordained of God.
6. Bring forth fruit—soul winners.
7. Ask the Father in Jesus' name.
8. To receive, we must keep his commandments.
9. Love one another.

Christ is to man:
1. Unchangeable—He loved them unto the end.

John 13:1
1   Now before the feast of the Passover, when Jesus knew that his hour was come that he should depart out of this world unto the Father, having loved his own which were in the world, he loved them unto the end.

2. Divine—Like a Father's love.

John 15:9
9   As the Father hath loved me, so have I loved you: continue ye in my love.

3. Self-Sacrificing—He laid down his life for us.

John 15:13
13   Greater love hath no man than this, that a man lay down his life for his friends.

4. Inseparable—Nothing can separate.

Romans 8:35
35   Who shall separate us from the love of Christ? Shall tribulation, or distress, or persecution, or famine, or nakedness, or peril, or sword?

5. Constraining—that the love of Christ.

2 Corinthians 5:14
14   For the love of Christ constraineth us: because we thus judge, that if one died for all, then were all dead:

      6. Sacrificial—Christ lives in me.

Galatians 2:20
20   I am crucified with Christ: nevertheless I live: yet not I, but Christ liveth in me: and the life which I now live in the flesh I live by the faith of the Son of God, who loved me, and gave himself for me.

      7. Manifested by His death—He laid down his life for us.

1 John 3:16
16   Hereby perceive we the love of God, because he laid down his life for us: and we ought to lay down our lives for the brethren.

Each of us must get closer to God through our relationship with Christ Jesus. Matthew 20:1-16 talks about the laborers in the vineyard.

Matthew 20:1-16
1   For the kingdom of heaven is like unto a man that is an householder, which went out early in the morning to hire labourers into his vineyard.
2   And when he had agreed with the labourers for a penny a day, he sent them into his vineyard.
3   And he went out about the third hour, and saw others standing idle in the marketplace,
4   And said unto them; Go ye also into the vineyard, and whatsoever is right I will give you. And they went their way.

5   Again he went out about the sixth and ninth hour, and did likewise.
6   And about the eleventh hour he went out, and found others standing idle, and saith unto them, Why stand ye here all the day idle?
7   They say unto him, Because no man hath hired us. He saith unto them, Go ye also into the vineyard; and whatsoever is right, that shall ye receive.
8   So when even was come, the lord of the vineyard saith unto his steward, Call the labourers, and give them their hire, beginning from the last unto the first.
9   And when they came that were hired about the eleventh hour, they received every man a penny.
10   But when the first came, they supposed that they should have received more; and they likewise received every man a penny.
11   And when they had received it, they murmured against the goodman of the house,
12   Saying, These last have wrought but one hour, and thou hast made them equal unto us, which have borne the burden and heat of the day.
13   But he answered one of them, and said, Friend, I do thee no wrong: didst not thou agree with me for a penny?
14   Take that thine is, and go thy way: I will give until the last, even as unto thee.
15   Is it not lawful for me to do what I will with mine own? Is thine eye evil, because I am good?
16   So the last shall be first, and the first last: for many be called, but few chosen.

This next parable tells of the Marriage's Guest. Both parables tell us of a friendship with God—"For many are called, but few are chosen."

Matthew 22:1-14

1   And Jesus answered and spake unto them again by parables, and said,
2   The kingdom of heaven is like unto a certain king, which made a marriage for his son,
3   And sent forth his servants to call them that were bidden to the wedding: and they would not come.
4   Again, he sent forth other servants, saying, Tell them which are bidden, Behold, I have prepared my dinner: my oxen and my fatlings are killed, and all things are ready: come unto the marriage.
5   but they made light of it, and went their ways, one to his farm, another to his merchandise:
6   And the remnant took his servants, and entreated them spitefully, and slew them.
7   But when the king heard thereof, he was wroth: and he sent forth his armies, and destroyed those murderers, and burned up their city.
8   Then saith he to his servants, The wedding is ready, but they which were bidden were not worthy.
9   Go ye therefore into the highways, and as many as ye shall find, bid to the marriage.
10   So those servants went out into the highways, and gathered together all as many as they found, both bad and good: and the wedding was furnished with guests.
11   And when the king came in to see the guests, he saw there a man which had not on a wedding garment:
12   And he saith unto him, Friend, how camest thou in hither not having a wedding garment? And he was speechless.
13   Then said the king to the servants, Bind him hand and foot, and take him away, and cast him into outer darkness; there shall be weeping and gnashing of teeth.
14   For many are called, but few are chosen.

8. Has God chosen you to be His friend? If not, draw closer to Him and keep His commandments.

9. Love one another, then He will choose you as His friend. John 15:16 says:

John 15:16
16   Ye have not chosen me, but I have chosen you, and ordained you, that ye should go and bring forth fruit, and that your fruit should remain: that whatsoever ye shall ask of the Father in my name; he may give it you.

Whatever You Do, Be Like Jesus

You hear in the news about humans taking matters into their own hands. In a way, they are "playing God."

If you want to be like Jesus, lose your ego, and follow God. Act as a servant with gratitude and humility. Jesus was not about his own glory. He was about manifesting God's glory through Him.

John 3:16
16   For God so loved the world, that he gave his only begotten Son, that whosoever believeth in him should not perish, but have everlasting life.

Jesus is the light in the world. If you want to be like Jesus, bring your truth and your light. Anything you do with these things in mind will be done with God by your side. Just like Jesus.

Sermon Outline

If you want to be me—Be me. If you want to be you—Be you. **But** whatever you do, be like Jesus, cause He's the One!

1 John 3:1-3
1   Behold, what manner of love the Father hath bestowed upon us, that we should be called the sons of God: therefore the world knoweth us not, because it knew him not.
2   Beloved, now are we the sons of God, and it doth not yet appear what we shall be: but we know that, when he shall appear, we shall be like him; for we shall see him as he is.
3   And every man that hath this hope in him purifieth himself, even as he is pure.

How do you be like Jesus?

1 Corinthians 15:34
34   Awake to righteousness, and sin not; for some have not the knowledge of God; I speak this to your shame.

Wow! That is powerful! **Sin not.** But I am ME—and you are YOU. So, how do you and I get to be like Jesus?

But—whatever you do, be like Jesus. He's the One!

Colossians 3:10
10   And have put on the new man, which is renewed in knowledge after the image of him that created him:

Let this mind be in you.

Philippians 2:5-8
5   *Let this mind be in you, which was also in Christ Jesus:*
6   *Who, being in the form of God, thought it not robbery to be equal with God:*
7   *But made himself of no reputation, and took upon him the form of a servant, and was made in the likeness of men:*
8   *And being found in fashion as a man, he humbled himself, and became obedient unto death, even the death of the cross.*

Well, if you want to be me…

Galatians 2:20
20   *I am crucified with Christ: nevertheless I live; not I, but Christ liveth in <u>me</u>: and the life which I now live in the flesh I live by the faith of the Son of God, who loved me, and gave himself for me.*

If you want to be you! Well, be you! But whatever you do, just know:

Ephesians 4:25-32
25   *Wherefore putting away lying, speak every man truth with is neighbour: for we are members one of another.*
26   *Be ye angry, and sin not: let not the sun go down upon your wrath:*
27   *Neither give place to the devil.*
28   *Let him that stole steal no more: but rather let him labour, working with his hands the thing which is good, that he may have to give to him that needeth.*

29   Let no corrupt communication proceed out of your mouth, but that which is good to the use of edifying, that it may minister grace unto the hearers.
30   And grieve not the holy Spirit of God, whereby ye are sealed unto the day of redemption.
31   Let all bitterness, and rath, and anger, and clamour, and evil speaking, be put away from you, with all malice:
32   And be ye kind one to another tenderhearted, forgiving one another, even as God for Christ's sake hath forgiven you.

But whatever you do, Be like Jesus—cause He's the One!

Ephesians 4:13
13   Till we all come in the unity of the faith, and of the knowledge of the Son of God, unto a perfect man, unto the measure of the stature of the fullness of Christ:

Small Words of Jesus

There are moments in the Bible, when Jesus speaks to his disciples or to the multitude. When he speaks, he is either telling stories with great lessons, revealing himself to his students, or inviting them to come and follow Him.

Sermon Outline

It is I.

Matthew 14:27
27   But straightaway Jesus spake unto them, saying, Be of good cheer; <u>it is I</u>; be not afraid.

Read the walking on the water story in Matthew 14:

Matthew 14:22-33
22   And straightway Jesus constrained his disciples to get into a ship, and to go before him unto the other side, while he sent the multitudes away.
23   And when he had sent the multitudes away, he went up into a mountain apart to pray: and when the evening was come, he was there alone.
24   But the ship was now in the midst of the sea, tossed with waves: for the wind was contrary.
25   And in the fourth watch of the night Jesus went unto them, walking on the sea.
26   And when the disciples saw him walking on the sea, they were troubled, saying, It is a spirit; and they cried out for fear.
27   But straightway Jesus spake unto them, saying, Be of good cheer; it is I: be not afraid.
28   And Peter answered him and said, Lord, if it be thou, bid me come unto thee on the water.
29   And he said, Come. And when Peter was come down out of the ship, he walked on the water, to go to Jesus.
30   But when he saw the wind boisterous, he was afraid; and begging to sink, he cried, saying, Lord, save me.

31   *And immediately Jesus stretched forth his hand, and caught him, and said unto him, O thou of little faith, wherefore didst thou doubt?*
32   *And when they were come into the ship, the wind ceased.*
33   *Then they that were in the ship came and worshipped him, saying, Of a truth thou art the Son*

Isaiah 52:6
6   *Therefore my people shall know my name: therefore they shall know in that day that I am he that doth speak: behold, <u>it is I</u>.*

Mark 6:50
50   *For they all saw him, and were troubled. And immediately he talked with them, and saith unto them, Be of good cheer: <u>it is I</u>; be not afraid.*

Luke 24:39
39   *Behold my hands and my feet, that <u>it is I</u> myself: handle me, and see; for a spirit hath not flesh and bones, as ye see me have.*

John 6:20
20   *But he saith unto them, <u>it is I</u>; be not afraid.*

Come.

Matthew 4:19
19   *And he saith unto them, <u>Follow me</u>, and I will make you fishers of men.*

Mark 1:17
17   *And Jesus said unto them, <u>Come ye after me</u>, and I will make you to become fishers of men.*

Mark 1:25
25   And Jesus rebuked him, saying, Hold thy peace, and *come out of him*.

Mark 10:14
14   But when Jesus saw it, he was much displeased, and said unto them, Suffer the little children to *come unto me*, and forbid them not: for of such is the kingdom of God.

John 7:37
37   In the last day, that great day of the feast, Jesus stood and cried, saying, If any man thirst, *let him come unto me*, and drink.

John 8:21
21   Then said Jesus again unto them, I go my way, and ye shall seek me, and shall die in your sins: whither I do, *ye cannot come*.

John 11:43
43   And when he thus had spoken, he cried with a loud voice, *Lazarus, come forth*.

John 17:1
1   These words spake Jesus, and lifted up his eyes to heaven, and said, *Father, the hour is come*; glorify thy Son, that thy Son also may glorify thee:

John 21:12
12   Jesus saith unto them, *Come and dine*. And none of the disciples durst ask him, Who art thou? knowing that it was the Lord.

Jesus is still saying, "<u>It is I</u>," so come on!

Appendix

Selected Scriptures
(King James Version)

Genesis 1:1
1   In the beginning God created the heaven and the earth.

Genesis 2:18
18   And the Lord God said, It is not good that the man should be alone; I will make him an help meet for him.

Genesis 2:21-25
21   And the Lord God caused deep sleep to fall upon Adam and he slept: and he took one of his ribs, and closed up the flesh instead thereof;
22   And the rib, which the Lord God had taken from man, made he a woman, and brought her unto the man.
23   And Adam said, This is now the bone of my bones, and flesh of my flesh: she shall be called Woman, because she was taken out of Man.
24   Therefore shall a man leave his father and his mother, and shall cleave unto his wife: and they shall be one flesh.
25   And they were both naked, the man and his wife, and were not ashamed.

Genesis 3:8
8   And they heard the voice of the Lord God walking in the garden in the cool of the day: and Adam and his wife hid themselves from the presence of the Lord God amongst the trees of the garden.

Genesis 3:15
15   And I will put my enmity between thee and the woman, and between thy seen and her seed; it shall bruise thy head, and thou shalt bruise his heel.

Genesis 12:3
3	And I will bless them that bless thee, and curse him that curseth thee: and in thee shall all families of the earth be blessed.

Genesis 15:1
1	After these things the word of the Lord came unto Abram in a vision, saying, Fear not, Abram: I am thy shield, and thy exceeding great reward.

Exodus 3:12
12	And he said, Certainly I will be with thee; and this shall be a token unto thee, that I have sent the: When thou hast brought forth the people out of Egypt, ye shall serve God upon this mountain.

Number 20:8
8	Take the rod, and gather thou the assembly together, thou, and Aaron thy brother, and speak ye unto the rock before their eyes; and it shall give forth his water, and thou shalt bring forth to them water out of the rock: so thou shalt give the congregation and their beasts drink.

Leviticus 11:44-45
44	For I am the Lord your God: ye shall therefore sanctify yourselves, and ye shall be holy; for I am holy: neither shall ye defile yourselves with any manner of creeping thing that creepeth upon the earth.
45	For I am the Lord that bringeth you up out of the land of Egypt, to be your God: ye shall therefore be holy, for I am holy.

1 Samuel 2:9a
9	He will keep the feet of his saints, and the wicked shall be silent in darkness; for by strength shall no man prevail.

1 Samuel 16:1

16   And the Lord said unto Samuel, How long wilt thou mourn for Saul, seeing I have rejected him from reigning over Israel? fill thine horn with oil, and go, I will send thee to Jesse the Bethlehemite: for I have provided me a king among his sons.

1 Samuel 16:12-13

12   And he sent, and brought him in. Now he was ruddy, and withal of a beautiful countenance, and goodly to look to. And the Lord said, Arise, anoint him: for this is he.

13   Then Samuel took the horn of oil, and anointed him in the midst of his brethren: and the spirit of the Lord came upon David from that day forward. So Samuel rose up, and went to Ramah.

2 Samuel 15:4

4   Absalom said moreover, Oh that I were made judge in the land, that every man which hath any suit or cause might come unto me, and I would do him justice!

2 Samuel 22:1-29 (David's Thanksgiving)

1   And David spake unto the Lord the words of this song in the day that the Lord had delivered him out of the hand of all his enemies, and out of the hand of Saul;

2   And he said, The Lord is my rock, and my fortress, and my deliverer;

3   The God of my rock; in him will I trust: he is my shield, and the horn of my salvation, my high tower, and my refuge, my saviour; thou savest me from violence.

4   I will call on the Lord, who is worthy to be praised: so shall I be saved from mine enemies.

5   When the waves of death compassed me, the floods of ungodly men made me afraid;

6   The sorrows of hell compassed me about; the snares of death prevented me;
7   In my distress I called upon the Lord, and cried to my God: and he did hear my voice out of his temple, and my cry did enter into his ears.
8   Then the earth shook and trembled; the foundations of heaven moved and shook, because he was wroth.
9   There went up a smoke out of his nostrils, and fire out of his mouth devoured: coals were kindled by it.
10   He bowed the heavens also, and came down; and darkness was under his feet.
11   And he rode upon a cherub, and did fly: and he was seen upon the wings of the wind.
12   He was made darkness pavilions round about him, dark waters, and thick clouds of the skies.
13   Through the brightness before him were coals of fire kindled.
14   The Lord thundered from heaven, and the most High uttered his voice.
15   And he sent out arrows, and scattered them; lightning, and discomfited them.
16   And the channels of the sea appeared, the foundations of the world were discovered, at the rebuking of the Lord, at the blast of the breath of his nostrils.
17   He sent from above, he took me; he drew me out of many waters;
18   He delivered me from my strong enemy, and from them that hated me: for they were too strong for me.
19   They prevented me in the day of my calamity: but the Lord was my stay.
20   He brought me forth also into a large place: he delivered me, because he delighted in me.
21   The Lord rewarded me according to my righteousness: according to the cleanness of my hands hath he recompensed me.

22   For I have kept the ways of the Lord, and have not wickedly departed from my God.
23   For all his judgments were before me: and as for his statutes, I did not depart from them.
24   I was also upright before him, and have kept myself from mine iniquity.
25   Therefore the Lord hath recompensed me according to my righteousness; according to my cleanness in his eye sight.
26   With the merciful thou wilt show thyself merciful, and with the upright man thou wilt show thyself upright.
27   With the pure thou wilt show thyself pure; and with the forward thou wilt show thyself unsavoury.
28   And the afflicted people thou wilt save: but thine eyes are upon the haughty, that thou mayest bring them down.
29   For thou art my lamp, O Lord: and the Lord will lighten m darkness.

Psalm 17:7
7   Show thy marvelous lovingkindness, O thou that savest by thy right hand them which put their trust in thee from those that rise up against them.

Psalm 19:5
5   Which is as a bridegroom coming out of his chamber, and rejoiceth as a strong man to run a race.

Psalm 19:14
14   Let the words of my mouth, and the meditation of my heart, be acceptable in thy sight, O Lord, my strength, and my redeemer.

Psalm 33:11
11   The counsel of the Lord standeth for ever, the thoughts of his heart to all generations.

Psalm 40:1
1   I waited patiently for the Lord; and he inclined unto e, and heard my cry.

Psalm 40:2
2   He brought me up also out of an horrible pit, out of the miry clay, and set my feet upon a rock, and established my goings.

Psalm 40:8-10
8   I delight to do thy will, O my God: yea, thy law is within my heart.
9   I have preached righteousness in the great congregation: lo, I have not refrained my lips, O Lord, thou knowest.
10   I have not hid thy righteousness within my heart: I have declared thy faithfulness and thy salvation: I have not concealed thy lovingkindness and thy truth from the great congregation.

Psalm 43:3
3   O send out thy light and thy truth: let them lead me; let them bring me unto thy holy hill, and to thy tabernacles.

Psalm 43:4
4   Then I will go unto the altar of God, unto God my exceeding joy: yea, upon the harp will I praise thee, O God my God.

Psalm 43:5
5   Why art thou cast down, O my soul? and why art thou disquieted within me? hope in God: for I shall yet praise him, who is the health of my countenance, and my God.

Psalm 119:105
105   Thy word is a lamp unto my feed, and a light unto my path.

Proverbs 6:16-19

16 These six things doth the Lord hate: yea, seven are an abomination unto him:

17 A proud look, a lying tongue, and hands that shed innocent blood,

18 An heart that deviseth wicked imaginations, feet that be swift in running to mischief,

19 A false witness that speaketh lies, and he that soweth discord among brethren.

Proverbs 18:22

22 Whoso findeth a wife findeth a good thing, and obtaineth favour of the Lord.

Isaiah 1:18-20

18 Come now, and let us reason together, saith the Lord: though your sins be as scarlet, they shall be as white as snow; though they be red like crimson, they shall be as wool.

19 If ye be willing and obedient, ye shall eat the good of the land:

20 But if ye refuse and rebel, ye shall be devoured with the sword: for the mouth of the Lord hath spoken it.

Isaiah 1:21

21 How is the faithful city become an harlot! It was full of judgment; righteousness lodged in it; but now murderers.

Isaiah 9:6

6 For us a child is born, unto us a son is given: and the government shall be upon his shoulder: and his name shall be called Wonderful, Counsellor, The mighty God, The everlasting Father, the Prince of Peace.

Isaiah 11:1-5

1   And there shall come forth a rod out of the stem of Jesse, and a Branch shall grow out of his roots:
2   And the spirit of the Lord shall rest upon him, the spirit of wisdom and understanding, the spirit of counsel and might, the spirit of knowledge and of the fear of the Lord;
3   And shall make him of quick understanding in the fear of the Lord: and he shall not judge after the sight of his eyes, neither reprove after the hearing of his ears:
4   But with righteousness shall he judge the poor, and reprove with equity for the meek of the earth: and he shall smite the earth with the rod of his mouth, and with the breath of his lips shall he slay the wicked.
5   And righteousness shall be the girdle of his loins, and faithfulness the girdle of his reins.

Isaiah 52:1-6

1   Awake, awake: put on thy strength, O Zion; put on thy beautiful garments, O Jerusalem, the holy city: for henceforth there shall no more come into thee the uncircumcised and the unclean.
2   Shake thyself from the dust; arise, and sit down, O Jerusalem: loose thyself from the bands of thy neck, O captive daughter of Zion.
3   For thus saith the Lord, Ye have sold yourselves for nought; and ye shall be redeemed without money.
4   For thus saith the Lord God, My people went down aforetime into Egypt to sojourn there; and the Assyrian oppressed them without cause.
5   Now therefore, what have I here, saith the Lord, that my people is taken away for nought? They that rule over them make them to howl, saith the Lord; and my name continually everyday is blasphemed.

6   Therefore my people shall know my name: therefore they shall know in that day that I am he that doth speak: behold, it is I.

Isaiah 52:7
7   How beautiful upon the mountains are the feet that bringeth good tidings, that buplisheth peace; that bringeth good tidings of good, that publisheth salvation: that saith unto Zion, Thy God reineth!

Isaiah 53:1
1   Who hath believed our report? And to whom is the arm of the Lord revealed?

Isaiah 53:2-5
2   For he shall grow up before him as a tender plant, and as a root out of a dry ground: he hath no form nor comeliness; and when we shall see him, there is no beauty that we should desire him.
3   He is despised and rejected of men; a man of sorrows, and acquainted with grief: and we hid as it were our faces from him; he was despised and we esteemed him not.
4   Surely he hath borne our griefs, and carried our sorrows: yet we did esteem him stricken, smitten of God, and afflicted.
5   But he was wounded for our transgressions, he was bruised for our iniquities: the chastisement of our peace was upon him; and with his stripes we are healed.

Isaiah 54:5
5   For thy Maker is thine husband; the Lord of hosts is his name; and the Redeemer the Holy One of Israel; The God of the whole earth shall he be called.

Jeremiah 1:4
4   Then the word of the Lord came unto me, saying,

Jeremiah 1:11
11   Moreover the word of the Lord came unto me, saying, Jeremiah, what seest thou? And I said, I see a rod of an almond tree.

Jeremiah 37:17
17   Then Zedekiah the king sent, and took him out: and the king asked him secretly in his house, and said, Is there any word from the Lord? And Jeremiah said, There is: for, said he, thou shalt be delivered into the hand of the king of Babylon.

Daniel 3:23-25
23   And these three men, Shadrach, Meshach, and Abednego, fell down bound into the midst of the burning fiery furnace.
24   Then Nebuchadnezzar the king was astonished, and rose up in haste, and spake, and said unto his counselors, Did not we cast three men bound into the midst of the fire? They answered and said unto the king, True, O king.
25   He answered and said, Lo, I see four men loose, walking In the midst of the fire, and they have no hurt; and the form of the fourth is like the Son of God.

Daniel 6:22
22   My God hath sent his angel, and hath shut the lions' mouths, that they have not hurt me: forasmuch as before him innocency was found in me; and also before thee, O king, have I done no hurt.

Daniel 7:13-14

13   I saw in the night visions, and, behold, one like the Son of man came with the clouds of heaven, and came to the Ancient of days, and they brought him near before him.

14   And there was given him dominion, and glory, and a kingdom, that all people, nations, and languages, should serve him: his dominion is an everlasting dominion, which shall not be destroyed.

Hosea 2:19-20

19   And I will betroth thee unto me for ever; yea, I will betroth thee unto me in righteousness, and in judgment, and in lovingkindness, and in mercies.

20   I will even betroth thee unto me in faithfulness: and thou shalt know the Lord.

Jonah 2:1-10

1   Then Jonah prayed unto the Lord his God out of the fish's belly,

2   And I said, I cried by reason of mine affliction unto the Lord, and he heard me; out of the belly of hell cried I, and thou heardest my voice.

3   For thou hadst cast me into the deep, in the midst of the seas; and the floods compassed me about: all thy billows and thy waves passed over me.

4   Then I said, I am cast out of thy sight; yet I will look again toward thy holy temple.

5   The waters compassed me about, even to the soul: the depth closed me round about, the weeds were wrapped about my head.

6   I went down to the bottoms of the mountains; the earth with her bars was about me for ever: yet hast thou brought up my life from corruption, O Lord my God.

7   When my soul fainted within me I remembered the Lord: and my prayer came in unto thee, into thine holy temple.
8   They that observe lying vanities forsake their own mercy.
9   But I will sacrifice unto thee with the voice of thanksgiving; I will pay that that I have vowed. Salvation is of the Lord.
10   And the Lord spake unto the fish, and it vomited out Jonah upon the dry land.

Zechariah 3:8
8   Fear now, O Joshua the high priest, thou, and thy fellows that sit before thee: for they are men wondered at: for, behold, I will bring forth my servant the Branch.

Zechariah 6:12
12   And speak unto him, saying, Thus speaketh the Lord of hosts, saying, Behold the man whose name is The Branch; and he shall grow up out of his place, and he shall build the temple of the Lord:

Malachi 1:2
2   I have loved you, saith the Lord. Yet ye say, Wherein hast thou loved us? Was not Esau Jacob's brother? Saith the Lord: yet I loved Jacob,

Malachi 3:1
1   Behold, I will send my messenger, and he shall prepare the way before me: and the Lord, whom ye seek, shall suddenly come to his temple, even the messenger of the covenant, whom ye delight in: behold, he shall come, saith the Lord of hosts.

Malachi 3:6
6   For I am the Lord, I change not; therefore ye sons of Jacob are not consumed.

Matthew 1:23
23   Behold, a virgin shall be with child, and shall bring forth a son, and they shall call his name Emmanuel, which being interpreted is, God with us.

Matthew 1:25
25   And knew her not till she had brought forth her firstborn son: and he called his name Jesus.

Matthew 2:2
2   Saying, Where is he that is born King of the Jews? For we have seen his star in the east, and are come to worship him.

Matthew 2:6
6   And thou Bethlehem, in the land of Juda, art not the least among the princes of Juda: for our of thee shall come a Governor, that shall rule my people Israel.

Matthew 2:12
12   And being warned of God in a dream that they should not return to Herod, they departed into their own country another way.

Matthew 3:17
17   And lo a voice from heaven, saying, This is my beloved Son, in whom I am well pleased.

Matthew 4:18-19
18   And Jesus, walking by the sea of Galilee, saw two brethren, Simon called Peter, and Andrew his brother, casting a net into the sea: for they were fishers.
19   And he saith unto them, Follow me, and I will make you fishers of men.

Matthew 5:9
9   Blessed are the peacemakers: for they shall be called the children of God.

Matthew 5:11-14
11   Blessed are ye, when men shall revile you, and persecute you, and shall say all manner of evil against you falsely, for my sake.
12   Rejoice, and be exceeding glad: for great is your reward in heaven: for so persecuted they the prophets which were before you.
13   Ye are the salt of the earth: if the salt have lost his savour, wherewith shall it be salted? It is thenceforth good for nothing, but to be cast out, and to be todden under foot of men.
14   Ye are the light of the world. A city that is set on an hill cannot be hid.

Matthew 5:16
16   Let your light shine before men, that they may see your good works, and glorify your Father which is in heaven.

Matthew 7:7
7   Ask and it shall be given you; seek, and ye shall find; knock, and it shall be opened unto you:

Matthew 8:27
27   But the men marveled, saying, What manner of man is this, that even the winds and the sea obey him!

Matthew 11:27
27   All things are delivered unto me of my Father: and no man knoweth the Son, but the Father; neither knoweth any man the Father, save the Son, and he to whomsoever the Son will reveal him.

Matthew 13:1-35 (Parable of the Sower)

1   The same day went Jesus out of the house, and sat by the sea side.

2   And great multitudes were gathered together unto him, so that he went into a ship, and sat; and the whole multitude stood on the shore.

3   And he spake many things unto them in parables, saying, Behold, a sower went forth to sow;

4   And when he sowed, some seeds fell by the way side, and the fowls came and devoured them up:

5   Some fell upon stony places, where they had not much earth: and forthwith they sprung up, because they had no deepness of earth:

6   And when the sun was up, they were scorched: and because they had no root, they withered away.

7   And some fell among the thorns; and the thorns sprung up, and choked them:

8   But other fell into good ground, and brought forth fruit, some an hundredfold, some sixtyfold, some thirtyfold.

9   Who hath ears to hear, let him hear.

10   And the disciples came, and said unto him, Why speakest thou unto them in parables?

11   He answered and said unto them, Because it is given unto you to know the mysteries of the kingdom of heaven, but to them it is not give,

12   For whosoever hath, to him shall be given, and he shall have more abundance: but whosoever hath not, from him shall be taken away even that he hath.

13   Therefore speak I to them in parables: because they seeing see not; and hearing they hear not, neither do they understand.

14   And in them is fulfilled the prophecy of Esaias, which saith, By hearing ye shall hear, and shall not understand; and seeing ye shall see, and shall not perceive:
15   For this people's heart is waxed gross, and their ears are dull of hearing, and their eyes they have closed; lest at any time they should see with their eyes and hear with their ears, and should understand with their heart, and should be converted, and I should heal them.
16   But blessed are your eyes, for they see: and your ears, for they hear.
17   For verily I say unto you, That many prophets and righteous men have desired to see those things which ye see, and have not seen them; and to hear those things which ye hear, and have not heard them.
18   Hear ye therefore the parable of the sower.
19   When any one heareth the word of the kingdom, and understandeth it not, then cometh the wicked one, and catcheth away that which was sown in his heart. This is he which received seed by the way side.
20   but he that received the seed into stony places, the same is he that heareth the word, and anon with joy receiveth it;
21   Yet hath he not root in himself, but dureth for a while: for when tribulation or persecution ariseth because of the word, by and by he is offended.
22   He also that received seed among the throns is he that heareth the word; and the care of this world, and the deceitfulness of riches, choke the word, and he becometh unfruitful.
23   But he that received seed into the good ground is he that heareth the word, and understandeth it; which also beareth fruit, and bringeth forth, some an hundrefod, some sixty, some thirty.
24   Another parable put he forth unto them, saying, The kingdom of heaven is likened unto a man which sowed good seed in his field:

25   But when the blade was sprung up, and brought forth fruit, then appeared the tares also.
27   So the servants of the householder came and said unto him, Sir, didst not thou sow good seed in thy field? From whence then hath it tares?
28   He said unto them, An enemy hath done this. The servants said unto him, Wilt thou then that we go and gather them up?
29   But he said, Nay; lest while ye gather up the tares, ye root up also the wheat with them.
30   Let both grow together until the harvest: and in the time of harvest I will say to the reapers, Gather ye together first the tares, and bind them in bundles to burn them: but gather the wheat into my barn.
31   Another parable put he forth unto them, saying, The kingdom of heaven is like to a grain of mustard seed, which a man took, and sowed in his field:
32   Which indeed is the least of all seeds: but when it is grown, it is the greatest among herbs, and becometh a tree, so that the birds of the air come and lodge in the branches thereof.
33   Antoher parable spake he unto them: The kingdom of heaven is like unto leaven, which a woman took, and hid in three measures a meal, till the wold was leavened.
34   All these things spake Jesus unto the multitude in parables; and without a parable spake he not unto them:
35   That it might might be fulfilled which was spoken by the prophet, saying, I will open my mouth in parables; I will utter things which have been kept secret from the foundation of the world.

Matthew 14:22-33
22   And straightway Jesus constrained his disciples to get into a ship, and to go before him unto the other side, while he sent the multitudes away.

23   And when he had sent the multitudes away, he went up into a mountain apart to pray: and when the evening was come, he was there alone.
24   But the ship was now in the midst of the sea, tossed with waves: for the wind was contrary.
25   And in the fourth watch of the night Jesus went unto them, walking on the sea.
26   And when the disciples saw him walking on the sea, they were troubled, saying, It is a spirit; and they cried out for fear.
27   But straightway Jesus spake unto them, saying, Be of good cheer; it is I: be not afraid.
28   And Peter answered him and said, Lord, if it be thou, bid me come unto thee on the water.
29   And he said, Come. And when Peter was come down out of the ship, he walked on the water, to go to Jesus.
30   But when he saw the wind boisterous, he was afraid; and begging to sink, he cried, saying, Lord, save me.
31   And immediately Jesus stretched forth his hand, and caught him, and said unto him, O thou of little faith, wherefore didst thou doubt?
32   And when they were come into the ship, the wind ceased.
33   Then they that were in the ship came and worshipped him, saying, Of a truth thou art the Son

Matthew 16:1-28

1   The Pharisees also with the Sadducees came, and tempting desired him that he would show them a sign from heaven.
2   He answered and said unto them, When it is evening, ye say, It will be fair weather: for the sky is red.
3   And in the morning, It will be foul weather to day: for the sky is red and lowering. O ye hypocrites, ye can discern the face of the sky; but can ye not discern the signs of the time?

4   A wicked and adulterous generation seeketh after a sign; and there shall no sign be given unto it, but the sign of the prophet Jonas. And he left them, and departed.
5   And when his disciples were come to the other side, they had forgotten to take bread.
6   Then Jesus said unto them, Take heed and beware of the leaven of the Pharisees of the Sadducees.
7   And they reasoned among themselves, saying, It is because we have taken no bread.
8   Which when Jesus perceived, he said unto them, O ye of little faith, why reason ye among yourselves, because ye have brought no bread?
9   Do ye not yet understand, neither remember the five loaves of the five thousand, and how many baskets ye took up?
10   Neither the seven loaves of the four thousand, and how many baskets ye took up?
11   How is it that ye do not understand that I spake it not to you concerning bread, that ye should beware of the leaven of the Pharisees and of the Sadducees?
12   Then understood they how that he bade them not beware of the leaven of bread, but of the doctrine of the Pharisees and of the Sadducees.
13   When Jesus came into the coasts of Caesarea Philippi, he asked his disciples, saying, Whom do men say that I the Son of man am?
14   And they said, Some say that thou art John the Baptist: some, Elias; and others, Jeremias, or one of the prophets.
15   He saith unto the, But whom say ye that I am?
16   And Simon Peter answered and said, Thou art the Christ, the Son of the living God.
17   And Jesus answered and said unto him, Blessed art thou, Simon Barjona: for flesh and blood hath not revealed it unto thee, but my Father which is in heaven.

18   And I say also unto thee, That thou art Peter, and upon this rock I will build my church; and the gates of hell shall not prevail against it.

19   And I will give unto thee that keys of the kingdom of heaven: and whatsoever thou shalt bind on earth shall be bound in heaven: and whatsoever thou shalt bind on earth shall be bound in heaven: and whatsoever thou shalt loose on earth shall be loosed in heaven.

20   Then charged he his disciples that they should tell no man that he was Jesus the Christ.

21   From that time forth began Jesus to show unto his disciples, how that he must go unto Jerusalem, and suffer many things of the elders and chief priests and scribes, and be killed, and be raised again the third day.

22   Then Peter took him, and began to rebuke him, saying, Be it far from thee, Lord: this shall not be unto thee.

23   But he turned, and said unto Peter, Get thee behind me, Satan: thou art an offence unto me: for thou savourest not the things that be of God, but those that be of men.

24   Then said Jesus unto his disciples, If any man will come after me, let him deny himself, and take up his cross, and follow me.

25   For whatsoever will save his life shall lose it: and whatsoever will lose his life for my sake shall find it.

26   For what is a man profited, if he shall gain the whole world, and lose his own soul? or what shall a man give in exchange for his soul?

27   For the Son of man shall come in the glory of his Father with his angels; and then he shall reward every man according to his works.

28   Verily I say unto you, There be some standing here, which shall not taste of death, till they see the Son of man coming in his kingdom.

Matthew 16:24
24   Then said Jesus to his disciples, if any man will come after me, let him deny himself, ad take up his cross, and follow me.

Matthew 17:5
5   While he yet spake, behold, a bright cloud overshadowed them: and behold a voice out of the cloud, which said, This is my beloved Son, in whom I am well pleased; hear ye him.

Matthew 19:3-6
3   The Pharisees also came unto him, tempting him, and saying unto him, Is is lawful for a man to put away his wife for every cause?
4   And he answered and said unto them, Have ye not read, that he which made them at the beginning made them male and female,
5   And said, For this cause shall a man leave father and other, and shall cleave to his wife: and they twain shall be one flesh?
6   Wherefore they are no more twain, but one flesh. What therefore God hath joined together, let not man put asunder.

Matthew 19:30
30   But many that are first shall be last; and the last shall be first.

Matthew 20:1-16 (The Laborers in the Vineyard)
1   For the kingdom of heaven is like unto a man that is an householder, which went out early in the morning to hire labourers into his vineyard.
2   And when he had agreed with the labourers for a penny a day, he sent them into his vineyard.

3   And he went out about the third hour, and saw others standing idle in the marketplace,

4   And said unto them; Go ye also into the vineyard, and whatsoever is right I will give you. And they went their way.

5   Again he went out about the sixth and ninth hour, and did likewise.

6   And about the eleventh hour he went out, and found others standing idle, and saith unto them, Why stand ye here all the day idle?

7   They say unto him, Because no man hath hired us. He saith unto them, Go ye also into the vineyard; and whatsoever is right, that shall ye receive.

8   So when even was come, the lord of the vineyard saith unto his steward, Call the labourers, and give them their hire, beginning from the last unto the first.

9   And when they came that were hired about the eleventh hour, they received every man a penny.

10   But when the first came, they supposed that they should have received more; and they likewise received every man a penny.

11   And when they had received it, they murmured against the goodman of the house,

12   Saying, These last have wrought but one hour, and thou hast made them equal unto us, which have borne the burden and heat of the day.

13   But he answered one of them, and said, Friend, I do thee no wrong: didst not thou agree with me for a penny?

14   Take that thine is, and go thy way: I will give until the last, even as unto thee.

15   Is it not lawful for me to do what I will with mine own? Is thine eye evil, because I am good?

16   So the last shall be first, and the first last: for many be called, but few chosen.

Matthew 20:29-34

29   And as they departed from Jericho, a great multitude followed him.

30   And, behold, two blind men sitting by the way side, when they heard that Jesus passed by, cried out, saying, Have mercy on us, O Lord, thou son of David.

31   And the multitude rebuked them, because the should hold their peace: but they cried the more, saying, Have mercy on us, O Lord, thou son of David.

32   And Jesus stood still, and called them, and said, What will ye that I shall do unto you?

33   They say unto him, Lord, that our eyes may be opened.

34   So Jesus had compassion on them, and touched their eyes: and immediately their eyes received sight, and they followed him.

Matthew 22:1-14 (The Marriage of the King's Son)

1   And Jesus answered and spake unto them again by parables, and said,

2   The kingdom of heaven is like unto a certain king, which made a marriage for his son,

3   And sent forth his servants to call them that were bidden to the wedding: and they would not come.

4   Again, he sent forth other servants, saying, Tell them which are bidden, Behold, I have prepared my dinner: my oxen and my fatlings are killed, and all things are ready: come unto the marriage.

5   but they made light of it, and went their ways, one to his farm, another to his merchandise:

6   And the remnant took his servants, and entreated them spitefully, and slew them.

7   But when the king heard thereof, he was wroth: and he sent forth his armies, and destroyed those murderers, and burned up their city.

8   Then saith he to his servants, The wedding is ready, but they which were bidden were not worthy.
9   Go ye therefore into the highways, and as many as ye shall find, bid to the marriage.
10   So those servants went out into the highways, and gathered together all as many as they found, both bad and good: and the wedding was furnished with guests.
11   And when the king came in to see the guests, he saw there a man which had not on a wedding garment:
12   And he saith unto him, Friend, how camest thou in hither not having a wedding garment? And he was speechless.
13   Then said the king to the servants, Bind him hand and foot, and take him away, and cast him into outer darkness; there shall be weeping and gnashing of teeth.
14   For many are called, but few are chosen.

Matthew 25:1-13 (Wise and Foolish Maidens)
1   Then shall the kingdom of heaven be likened unto ten virgins, which took their lamps, and went forth to meet the bridegroom.
2   And five of them were wise, and five were foolish.
3   They that were foolish took their lamps, and took no oil with them:
4   but the wise took oil in their vessels with their lamps.
5   While the bridegroom tarried, they all slumbered and slept.
6   And at midnight there was a cry made, Behold, the bridegroom cometh; go ye out to meet him.
7   Then all those virgins arose, and trimmed their lamps.
8   And the foolish said unto the wise, Give us of your oil; for our lamps are gone out.
9   but the wise answered, saying, Not so; lest there be not enough for us and you: but go ye rather to them that sell, and buy for yourselves.

10   And while they went to buy, the bridegroom came; and they that were ready went in with him to the marriage: and the door was shut.
11   Afterward came also the other virgins, saying, Lord, Lord, open to us.
12   But he answered and said, Verily I say unto you, I know you not.
13   Watch therefore, for ye know neither the day nor the hour wherein the Son of man cometh.

Matthew 26 (Judas Betrays Christ)
1   And it came to pass, when Jesus had finished all these sayings, he said unto his disciples,
2   Ye know that after two days is the feast of the Passover, and the Son of the man is betrayed to be crucified.
3   Then assembled together the chef priests, and the scribes, and the elders of the people, unto the palace of the high priest, who was called Caiaphas,
4   And consulted that they might take Jesus by subtlety, and kill him.
5   But they said, Not on the feast day, lest there be an uproar among the people.
6   Now when Jesus was in Bethany, in the house of Simon the leper,
7   There came unto him a woman having an alabaster box of very precious ointment, and poured it on his head, as he said at meat.
8   But when his disciples saw it, they had indignation, saying, To what purpose is this waste?
9   For this ointment might have been sold for much, and given to the poor.
10   When Jesus understood it, he said unto them, Why trouble ye the woman? For she hath wrought a good work upon me.

11   For ye have the poor always with you; but me ye have not always.

12   For in that she hath poured this ointment on my body, she did it for my burial.

13   Verily I say unto you, Wheresoever this gospel shall be preached in the whole world, there shall also this, that this woman hath done, be told for a memorial of her.

14   Then one of the twelve, called Judas Iscariot, went unto the chief priests,

15   And said unto them, What will ye give me, and I will deliver him unto you? And they covenanted with him for thirty pieces of silver.

16   And from that time he sought opportunity to betray him.

17   Now the first day of the feast of unleavened bread the disciples came to Jesus, saying unto him, Where will thou that we prepare for thee to eat the passover?

18   And he said, Go into the city to such a man, and say unto him, The Master saith, My time is at hand; I will keep the passover, at thy house with my disciples.

19   And the disciples did as Jesus had appointed them; and they made ready the passover.

20   Now when the even was come, he sat down with the twelve.

21   And as they did eat, he said, Verily I say unto you, that one of you shall betray me.

22   And they were exceeding sorrowful, and began every one of them to say unto him, Lord, is it I?

23   And he answered and said, He that dippeth his hand with me in the dish, the same shall ye betray me.

24   The Son of man goeth as it is written of him: but woe unto that man by whom the Son of man is betrayed! It had been good for that man if he had not been born.

25   Then Judas, which betrayed him, answered and said, Master, is it I? He said unto him, Thou hast said.

26   And as they were eating, Jesus took bread, and blessed it, and brake it, and gave it to the disciples, and said, Take, eat; this is my body.
27   And he took the cup, and gave thanks, and gave it to them, saying, Drink ye all of it;
28   For this is my blood of the new testament, which is shed for many for the remission of sins.
29   But I say unto you, I will not drink henceforth of this fruit of the vine, until that day when I drink it new with you in my Father's kingdom.
30   And when they had sung an hymn, they went out into the mount of Olives.
31   Then saith Jesus unto them, All ye shall be offended because of me this night: for it is written, I will smite the shepherd, and the sheep of the flock shall be scattered abroad.
32   But after I am risen again, I will go before you in Galilee.
33   Peter answered and said unto him, Though all men shall be offended because of thee, yet will I never be offended.
34   Jesus said unto him, Verily I say unto thee, That this night, before the cock crow, thou shalt deny me thrice.
35   Peter said unto him, Though I should die with thee, yet will I not deny thee. Likewise also said all the disciples.
36 Then cometh Jesus with them unto a place called Gethsemane, and saith unto the disciples, Sit ye here, while I go and pray yonder.
37   And he took with him Peter and the two sons of Zebedee, and began to be sorrowful and very heavy.
38   Then saith he unto them, My soul is exceeding sorrowful, even unto death: tarry ye here, and watch with me.
39   And he went a little farther, and fell on his face, and prayed, saying, O my Father, if it be possible, let this cup pass form me: nethertheless not as I will, but as thou wilt.

40   And he cometh unto the disciples, and findeth them asleep, and saith unto Peter, What, could ye not watch with me one hour?
41   Watch and pray, that ye enter not into temptation: the spirit indeed is swilling, but the flesh is weak.
42   He went away again the second time, and prayed, saying O my Father, if this cup may not pass away from me, except I drink it, thy will be done.
43   And he came and found them asleep again: for their eyes were heavy.
44   And he left them, and went away again, and prayed the third time, saying the same words.
45   Then cometh he to his disciples, and saith unto them, Sleep on now, and take your rest: behold, the hour is at hand, and the Son of man is betrayed into the hands of sinners.
46   Rise, let us be going: behold, he is at the hand that doth betray me.
47   And while he yet spake, lo, Judas, one of the twelve, came, and with him a great multitude with swords and staves, from the chief priests and elders of the people.
48   Now he that betrayed him gave them a sign, saying, Whomsoever I shall kiss, that same is he: hold him fast.
49   And forthwith he came to Jesus, and said, Hail, master; and kissed him.
50   And Jesus said unto him, Friend, wherefore art thou come?
51   And, behold, one of them which were with Jesus stretched out his hand, and drew his sword, and struck a servant of the high priest's, and smote off his ear.
52   Then said Jesus unto him, Put up again thy sword into his place: for all they that take the sword shall perish with the sword.
53   Thinkest thou that I cannot now pray to my Father, and he shall presently give me more than twelve legions of angels?

54   But how then shall the scriptures be fulfilled, that thus it must be?
55   In that same hour said Jesus to the multitudes, Are ye come out as against a thief with swords and staves for to take me? I sat daily with you teaching in the temple, and ye laid no hold on me.
56   But all this was done, that the scriptures of the prophets might be fulfilled. Then all the disciples forsook him, and fled.
57 And they that he had laid hold on Jesus led him away to Caiaphas the high priest, where the scribes and the elders were assembled.
58   But Peter followed him afar off unto the high priest's palace, and went in, and sat with the servants, to see the end.
59   Now the chief priests, and elders, and all the council, sought false witness against Jesus, to put him to death;
60   But found none: yea, though many false witnesses came, yet found they none. At the last came two false witnesses,
61   And said, This fellow said, I am able to destroy the temple of God, and to build it in three days.
62   And the high priest arose, and said unto him, Answerest thou nothing? What is it which these witness against thee?
63   But Jesus held his peace. And the high priest answered and said unto him, I adjure thee by the living God, that thou tell us whether thou be the Christ, the Son of God.
64   Jesus saith unto him, Thou hast said: nevertheless I say unto you, Hereafter shall ye see the Son of man sitting on the right hand of power, and coming in the clouds of heaven.
65   Then the high priest rent his clothes, saying, He hath spoken blasphemy; what further need have we of witnesses? Behold, now ye have heard his blasphemy.
66   What think ye? They answered and said, He is guilty of death.

67   Then did they spit in his face and buffeted him; and others smote him with the palms of their hands,
68   Saying, Prophesy unto us, thou Christ, Who is he that smote thee?
69   Now Peter sat without in the palace: and a damsel came unto him, saying, Thou also wast with Jesus of Galilee.
70   But he denied before them all, saying, I know not what thou sayest.
71   And when he was gone out into the porch, another maid saw him, and said unto them that were there, This fellow was also with Jesus of Nazareth.
72   And again he denied with an oath, I do not know the man.
73   And after a while came unto him they that stood by, and said to Peter, Surley thou also art one of them; for thy speech bewrayeth thee.
74   Then began he the curse and to swear, saying, I know not the man. And immediately the cock crew.
75   And Peter remembered the word of Jesus, which said unto him, Before the cock crow, thou shalt deny me thrice. And he went out, and wept bitterly.

Matthew 28:18
18   And Jesus came and spake unto them, saying, All power is given unto me in heaven and in earth.

Mark 1:17
17   And Jesus said unto them, Come ye after me, and I will make you to become fishers of men.

Mark 1:25
25   And Jesus rebuked him, saying, Hold thy peace, and come out of him.

Mark 6:50

50   For they all saw him, and were troubled. And immediately he talked with them, and saith unto them, Be of good cheer: *it is I; be not afraid.*

Mark 10:9

9   What therefore God hath joined together, let not man put asunder.

Mark 10:14

14   But when Jesus saw it, he was much displeased, and said unto them, Suffer the little children to come unto me, and forbid them not: for of such is the kingdom of God.

Mark 10:17-23

17   And when he was gone forth into the way, there came one running, and kneeled to him, Good master, what shall I do that I may inherit eternal life?
18   And Jesus said unto him, Why callest thou me good? There is none good but one, that is, God.
19   Thou knowest the commandments, Do not commit adultery, Do not kill, Do not steal, Do not bear false witness, Defraud not, Honour thy father and mother.
20   And he answered and said unto him, Master, all these have I observed form my youth.
21   Then Jesus beholding him loved him, and said unto him, One thing thou lackest: go thy way, sell whatsoever thou hast, and give to the poor, and thou shalt have treasure in heaven: and come, take up the cross, and follow me.
22   And he was sad at that saying, and went away grieved: for he had great possessions.
23   And Jesus looked round about, and saith unto his disciples, How hardly shall they that have riches enter into the kingdom of God!

Mark 10:28-30

28   Then peter began to say unto him, Lo, we have left all, and have followed thee.

29   And Jesus answered and said, Verily I say unto you, There is no man that hath left house, or brethren, or sisters, or father, or mother, or wife, or children, or lands, for my sake, and the gospel's,

30   But he shall receive an hundredfold now in this time, houses, and brethren, and sisters, and mothers, and children, and lands, with persecutions; and in the world to come eternal life.

Mark 10:46-52

46   And they came to Jericho, and as he went out of Jericho with his disciples and a great number of people, blind Bartimaeus, the son of Timaeus, sat by the highway side begging.

47   And when he heard that it was Jesus of Nazareth, he began to cry out, and say, Jesus, thou son of David, have mercy on me.

48   And many charged him that he should hold his peace: but he cried the more a great deal. Thou son of David have mercy on me.

49   And Jesus stood still, and commanded him to be called. And they call the blind man, saying unto him, Be of good comfort, rise; he calleth thee.

50   And he, casting away his garment, rose, and came to Jesus.

51   And Jesus answered and said unto him, What wilt thou that I should do unto thee? The blind man said unto him, Lord, that I might receive my sight.

52   And Jesus said unto him, Go thy way; thy faith hath made thee whole. And immediately he received his sight, and followed Jesus in the way.

Mark 13:10
10   And the gospel must first be published among all nations.

Mark 14:36
36   And he said, Abba, Father, all things are possible unto thee; take away this cup from me: nevertheless not what I will, but what thou wilt.

Mark 15:21-22
21   And they compel one Simon a Cyrenian, who passed by, coming out of the country, the father of Alexander and Rufus, to bear his cross.
22   And they bring him unto the place Golgotha, which is, being interpreted, The place of a skull.

Mark 19:23-24
23   And they give him to drink wine mingled with myrrh: but he received it not.
24   And when they had crucified him, they parted his garments, casting lots upon them, what every man should take.

Luke 1:26-31
26   And in the sixth month the angel Gabriel was sent from God unto a city of Galilee, named Nazareth.
27   To a virgin espoused to a man whose name was Joseph, of the house of David; and the virgin's name was Mary.
28   And the angel came in unto her, and said, Hail, thou that art highly favoured, the Lord is with thee: blessed art thou among women.
29   And when she saw him, she was troubled at his saying, and cast in her mind what manner of salutation this should be.
30   And the angel said unto her, Fear not, Mary: for thou hast found favour with God.

31   And, behold, thou shalt conceive in thy womb, and bring forth a son, and shalt call his name Jesus.

Luke 2:7
7   And she brought forth her first-born son, and wrapped him in swaddling clothes, and laid him in a manger; because there was no room for them in the inn.

Luke 2:40
40   And the child grew, and waxed strong in spirit, filled with wisdom: and the grace of God was upon him.

Luke 2:41-49 (Extraordinary Child)
41   Now his parents went to Jerusalem every year at the feast of the passover.
42   And when he was twelve years old, they went up to Jerusalem after the custom of the feast.
43   And when they had fulfilled the days, as they returned, the child Jesus tarried behind in Jerusalem; and Joseph and his mother knew not of it.
44   But they, supposing him to have been in the company, went a day's journey; and they sought him among their kinsfolk and acquaintance.
45   And when they found him not, they turned back again to Jerusalem, seeking him.
46   And it came to pass, that after three days they found him in the temple, sitting in the midst of the doctors, bother hearing them, and asking them questions.
47   And all that heard him were astonished at his understanding and answers.
48   And when they saw him, they were amazed: and his mother said unto him, Son, why hast thou thus dealt with us? Behold, thy father and I have sought thee sorrowing.

49   And he said unto them, How is that ye sought me? wist ye not that I must be about my Father's business?

Luke 11:34

34 The light of the body is the eye: therefore when thine eye is single, thy whole body also is full of light; but when thine eye is evil, thy body also is full of darkness.

Luke 12:1-5 (Covetousness to be Avoided)

1   In the mean time, when there were gathered together an innumerable multitude of people, insomuch that they trode one upon another, he began to say unto his disciples first of all, Beware ye of the leaven of the Pharisees, which is hypocrisy.
2   For there is nothing covered, that shall not be revealed; neither hid, that shall not be known.
3   Therefore whatsoever ye have spoken in darkness shall be heard in the light; and that which ye have spoken in the ear in closets shall be proclaimed upon the housetops.
4   And I say unto you my friends, Be not afraid of them that kill the body, and after that have no more that they can do.
5   But I will forewarn you whom ye shall fear: Fear him, which after he hath killed hath power to cast into hell; yea, I say unto you, Fear him.

Luke 14:25-33

25 And there went great multitudes with him: and he turned, and said unto them,
26 If any man come to me, and hate not his father, and mother, and wife, and children, and brethren, and sisters, yea, and his own life also, he cannot be my disciple.
27 And whosoever doth not bear his cross, and come after me, cannot be my disciple.

28   For which of you, intending to build a tower, sitteth not down first, and coutheth the cost, whether he have sufficient to finish it?
29   Lest haply, after he hath laid the foundation, and is not able to finish it, all that behold it begin to mock him,
30   Saying, This man began to build, and was not able to finish.
31   Or what king, going to make war against another king, sitteth not down first, and consulteth whether he be able with then thousand to meet him that cometh against him with twenty thousand?
32   Or else, while the other is yet a great way off, he sendeth an ambassage, and desireth conditions of peace.
33   So, likewise, whosoever he be of you that forsaketh not all that he hath, he cannot be my disciple.

Luke 15:11-19 (Three Parables of the Lost)

11   And he said, A certain man had two sons:
12   And the younger of them said to his father, Father, give me the portion of goods that falleth to me. And he divided unto them his living.
13   And not many days after the younger son gathered all together, and took his journey into a far country, and there wasted his substance with riotous living.
14   And when he had spent all, there arose a mighty famine in that land; and he began to be in want.
15   And he went and joined himself to a citizen of that country; and he sent him into his fields to feed swine.
16   And he would fain have filled his belly with the husks that the swine did eat: and no man gave unto him.
17   And when he came to himself, he said, How many hired servants of my father's have bread enough to apare, and I perish with hunger!

18   I will arise and go to my father, and will say unto him, Father, I have sinned against heaven, and before thee.
19   And am no more worthy to be called thy son: make me as one of thy hired servants.

Luke 15:25-32
25   Now his elder son was in the field: and as he came and drew nigh to the house, he heard music and dancing.
26   And he called one of the servants, and asked what these things meant.
27   And he said unto him, Thy brother is come; and thy father hath killed the fatted calf, because he hath received him safe and sound.
28   And he was angry, and would not go in: therefore came his father out, and entreated him.
29   And he answering said to his father, Lo, these many years do I serve thee, neither transgressed I at any time thy commandment: and yet thou never gavest me a kid, that I might make merry with my friends:
30   But as soon as this thy son was come, which hath devoured thy living with harlots, thou hast killed for him the fatted calf.
31   And he said unto him, Son, thou art ever with me, and all that I have in thine.
32   It was meet that we should make merry, and be glad: for this thy brother was dead, and is alive again; and was lost, and is found.

Luke 16:19-31 (Lazarus and "Dives")
19   There was a certain rich man, which was clothed in purple and fine linen, and fared sumptuously every day:
20   And there was a certain beggar named Lazarus, which was laid at his gate, full of sores,

21   And desiring to be fed with the crumbs which fell from the rich man's table: moreover the dogs came and licked his sores.
22   And it came to pass, that the beggar died, and was carried by the angels into Abraham's bosom: the rich man also died, and was buried:
23   And in hell he lift up his eyes, being in torments, and seeth Abraham afar off, and Lazarus in his bosom.
24   And he cried and said, Father Abraham, have mercy on me, and send Lazarus, that he may dip the tip of his finger in water, and cool my tongue; for I am tormented in this flame.
25   But Abraham said, Son, remember that thou in thy lifetime receivedst thy good things, and likewise Lazarus evil things: but now he is comforted, and thou art tormented.
26   And beside all this, between up and you there is a great gulf fixed: so that they which would pass from hence to you cannot; neither can they pass to us, that would come from thence.
27   Then he said, I pray thee therefore, father, that thou wildest send him to my father's house:
28   For I have five brethren; that he may testify unto them, lest they also come into this place of torment.
29   Abraham saith unto him, They have Moses and the prophets; let them hear them.
30   And he said, Nay, Father Abraham: but if one went unto them from the dead, they will repent.
31   And he said unto him, If they hear not Moses and the prophets, neither will they be persuaded though one rose from the dead.

Luke 18:35-43

35   And it came to pass, that as he was come nigh unto Jericho, a certain blind man sat by the way side begging:
36   And hearing the multitude pass by, he asked what it meant.
37   And they told him, that Jesus of Nazareth passeth by.

38 And he cried, saying, Jesus, thou son of David, have mercy on me.

39 And they which went before rebuked him, that he should hold his peace: but he cried so much the more. Thou son of David, have mercy on me.

40 And Jesus stood, and commanded him to be brought unto him: and when he was come near, he asked him.

41 Saying, What wilt thou that I shall do unto thee? And he said, Lord, that I may receive my sight.

42 And Jesus said unto him, Receive thy sight: thy faith hath saved thee.

43 And immediately he received his sight, and following him, florifying God: and all the people, when they saw it, gave praise unto God.

Luke 24:39
39 Behold my hands and my feet, that it is I myself: handle me, and see; for a spirit hath not flesh and bones, as ye see me have.

John 1:1-14 (The Divinity of Christ)
1 In the beginning was the Word, and the Word was with God, and the Word was God.

2 The same was in the beginning with God.

3 All things were made by him; and without him was not any thing made that was made.

4 In him was life; and the life was the light of men.

5 And the light shineth in darkness; and the darkness comprehended it not.

6 There was a man sent from God, whose name was John.

7 The same came for a witness, to bear witness of the Light, that all men through him might believe.

8 He was in the world, and the world was made by him, and the world knew him not.

9   That was the true Light, which lighteth every man that cometh into the world.
10   He was in the world, and the world was made by him, and the world knew him not.
11   He came unto his own, and his own received him not.
12   But as many as received him, to them gave he power to become the sons of God, even to them that believed on his name:
13   Which were born, not of blood, nor of the will of the flesh, nor of the will of man, but of God.
14   And the Word was made flesh, and dwelt among us, (and we beheld his glory, the glory as of the only begotten of the Father,) full of grace and truth.

John 1:26, 29
26   John answered them, saying, I baptize with water: but there standeth one among you whom ye know not;
29   The next day John seeth Jesus coming unto him, and saith, Behold the Lamb of God, which taketh away the sin of the world.

John 1:45-46
45   Philip findeth Nathanael, and saith unto him, We have found him, We have found him, of whom Moses in the law, and the prophets, did write, Jesus of Nazarreth, the son of Joseph.
46   And Nathanael said undo him, Can there any good thing come out of Nazareth? Philip saith unto him, Come and see.

John 3:1-10 (Necessity of Regeneration)
1   There was a man of the Pharisees, named Nicodemus, a ruler of the Jews:

2   The same came to Jesus by night, and said unto him, Rabbi, we know that thou art a teacher come from God: for no man can do these miracles that thou doest, except God be with him.
3   Jesus answered and said unto him, Verily, verily, I say unto thee, Except a man be born again, he cannot see the kingdom of God.
4   Nicodemus saith unto him, How can a man be born when he is old? can he enter the second time into his mother's womb, and be born?
5   Jesus answered, Verily, verily, I say unto thee, Except a man be born of water and of the Spirit, he cannot enter into the kingdom of God.
6   That which is born of the flesh is flesh; and that which is born of the Spirit is spirit.
7   Marvel not that I said unto thee, Ye must be born again.
8   The wind bloweth where it listeth, and thou hearest the sound thereof, but canst not tell whence it cometh, and whither it goeth: so is every one that is born of the Spirit.
9   Nicodemus answered and said unto him, How can these things be?
10 Jesus answered and said unto him, Art thou a master of Israel, and knowest not these things?

John 3:16-18
16 For God so loved the world, that he gave his only begotten Son, that whosoever believeth in him should not perish, but have everlasting life.
17 For God sent not his Son into the world to condemn the world; but that the world through him might be saved.
18 He that believeth on him is not condemned: but he that believeth not is condemned already, because he hath not believed in the name of the only begotten Son of God.

John 3:35
35   The Father loveth the Son, and hath given all things into his hand.

John 6:20
20   But he saith unto them, it is I; be not afraid.

John 7:6
6   Then Jesus said unto them, My time is not yet come: but your time is alway ready.

John 7:37
37   In the last day, that great day of the feast, Jesus stood and cried, saying, If any man thirst, let him come unto me, and drink.

John 8:21
21   Then said Jesus again unto them, I go my way, and ye shall seek me, and shall die in your sins: whither I do, ye cannot come.

John 8:58
58   Jesus said unto them, Verily, verily, I say unto you, Before Abraham was, I am.

John 10:1-11
1   Verily, verily, I say unto you, He that entereth not by the door into the sheepfold, but climbeth up some other way, the same is a thief and a robber.
2   But he that entereth in by the door is the shepherd of the sheep.
3   To him the porter openeth; and the sheep hear his voice: and he calleth his own sheep by name, and leadeth them out.

4	And when he putteth forth his own sheep, he goeth before them, and the sheep follow him: for they know his voice.
5	And a stranger will they not follow, but will flee from him: for they know not the voice of strangers.
6	This parable spake Jesus unto them: but they understood not what things they were which he spake unto them.
7	Then said Jesus unto them again, Verily, verily, I say unto you, I am the door of the sheep.
8	All that ever came before me are thieves and robbers: but the sheep did not hear them.
9	I am the door: by me if any man enter in, he shall be saved, and shall go in and out, and find pasture.
10	The thief cometh not, but for to steal, and to kill, and to destroy: I am come tha they might have life, and that they might have it more abundantly.
11	I am the good shepherd: the good shepherd giveth his life for the sheep.

John 10:14
14	I am the good shepherd, and know my sheep, and am known of mine.

John 10:30
30	I and my Father are one.

John 11:43
43	And when he thus had spoken, he cried with a loud voice, Lazarus, come forth.

John 13:1
1	Now before the feast of the Passover, when Jesus knew that his hour was come that he should depart out of this world unto the Father, having loved his own which were in the world, he loved them unto the end.

John 13:34-35

34 A new commandment I give unto you, That ye love one another; as I have loved you, that ye also love one another.

35 By this shall all men know that ye are my disciples, if ye have love to another.

John 14:1-21 (The Comforter Promised)

1 Let not your heart be troubled: ye believe in God, believe also in me.
2 In my Father's house are many mansions: if it were not so, I would have told you. I go to prepare a place for you.
3 And if I go and prepare a place for you, I will come again, and receive you unto myself: that where I am, there ye may be also.
4 And whither I go ye know, and the way ye know.
5 Thomas saith unto him, Lord, we know not whither thou goest; and how can we know the way?
6 Jesus saith unto him, I am the way, the truth, and the life: no man cometh unto the Father, but by me.
7 If ye had known me, ye should have known my Father also: and from henceforth ye know him, and have seen him.
8 Phillip saith unto him, Lord, show us the Father, and it sufficeth us.
9 Jesus saith unto him, Have I been so long time with you, and yet hast thou not known me, Philip? he that hath seen me hath seen the Father; and how savest thou then, Show us the Father?
10 Believest thou not that I am in the Father, and the Father in me? The words that I speak unto you I speak not of myself: but the Father that dwelleth in me, he doeth the works.

11   Believe me that I am in the Father, and the Father in me: or else believe me for the very works' sake.

12   Verily, verily, I say unto you, He that believeth on me, the works that I do shall he do also; and greater works than these shall he do; because I go unto my Father.

13   And whatsoever ye shall ask in my name, that will I do, that the Father may be glorified in the Son.

14   If ye shall ask any thing in my name, I will do it.

15   If ye love me, keep my commandments.

16   And I will pray the Father, and he shall give you another Comforter, that he may abide with you for ever;

17   Even the Spirit of truth; whom the world cannot receive, because it seeth him not, neither knoweth him: but ye know him; for he dwelleth with you, and shall be in you.

18   I will not leave you comfortless: I will come to you.

19   Yet a little while, and the world seeth me no more: but ye see me: because I live, ye shall live also.

20   At that day ye shall know that I am in my Father, and ye in me, and I in you.

21   He that hath my commandments, and keepeth them, he it is that loveth me: and he that loveth me shall be loved of my Father, and I will love him, and will manifest myself to him.

John 15:9

9   As the Father hath loved me, so have I loved you: continue ye in my love.

John 15:12-17

12   This is my commandment, That ye love one another, as I have loved you.

13   Greater love hath no man than this, that a man lay down his life for his friends.

14   Ye are my friends, if he do whatsoever I command you.

15   Henceforth I call you not servants: for the servant knoweth not what his lord doeth: but I have called you friends; for all things that I have heard of my Father I have made known unto you.
16   Ye have not chosen me, but I have chosen you, and ordained you, that ye should go and bring forth fruit, and that your fruit should remain: that whatsoever ye shall ask of the Father in my name, he may give it you.
17   These things I command you, that ye love one another.

John 15:24
24   If I had not done among them the works which none other man did, they had not had sin: but now have they both seen and hated both me and my Father.

John 16:5-14
5   But now I go my way to him that sent me; and none of you asketh me, Whither goest thou?
6   But because I have said these things unto you, sorrow hath filled your heart.
7   Nevertheless I tell you the truth; It is expedient for you that I go away; for if I go not away, the Comforter will not come unto you: but if I depart, I will send him unto you.
8   And when he is come, he will reprove the world of sin, and of righteousness, and of judgment:
9   Of sin, because they believe not on me;
10   Of righteousness, because I go to my Father, and ye see me no more;
11   Of judgment, because prince of this world is judged.
12   I have yet many things to say unto you, but ye cannot hear them now.

13 Howbeit when he, the Spirit of truth, is come, he will guide you into all truth: for he shall not speak of himself; but whatsoever he shall hear, that shall he speak: and he will show you things to come.
14 He shall glorify me: for he shall receive of mine, and shall show it unto you.

John 17:1
1 These words spake Jesus, and lifted up his eyes to heaven, and said, Father, the hour is come; glorify thy Son, that thy Son also may glorify thee:

John 17:11
11 And now, I am no more in the world, but these are in the world, and I come to thee. Holy Father, keep through thine own name those whom thou hast given me, that they make be one, as we are.

John 17:15-17
15 I pray not that thou shouldest take them out of the world, but that thou shouldest keep them from evil.
16 They are not of the world, even as I am not of the world.
17 Sanctify them through thy through: thy word is truth.

John 21:12
12 Jesus saith unto them, Come and dine. And none of the disciples durst ask him, Who art thou? knowing that it was the Lord.

Acts 1:4-8
4 And, being assembled together with them, but wait for the promise of the Father, which, saith he, ye have heard of me.
5 for John truly baptized with water; but ye shall be baptized with the Holy Ghost not many days hence.

6   When they therefore were come together, they asked of him, saying, Lord, wilt thou at this time restore again the kingdom of Israel?
7   And he said unto them, It is not for me to know the times of the seasons, which the Father hath put in his own power.
8   But ye shall receive power, after that the Holy Ghost is come upon you: and ye shall be witnesses unto me both in Jerusalem, and in all Judaea, and in Samaria, and unto the uttermost part of the earth.

Acts 2:1-4a
1   And when the day of Pentecost was fully come, they were all with one accord in one place.
2   And suddenly there came a sound from heaven as of a rushing mighty wind, and it filled all the house where they were sitting.
3   And there appeared unto them cloven tongues like as of fire, and it sat upon each of them.
4   And they were all filled with the Holy Ghost.

Acts 13:22-23
22   And when he had removed him, he raised up unto them David to be their king: so whom also he gave testimony, and said, I have found David the son of Jesse, a man after mine own heart, which shall fulfil all my will.
23   Of this man's seed hath God according to his promise raised unto Israel a Saviour, Jesus:

Acts 26:16 & 18
16   But rise, and stand upon thy feet: for I have appeared unto thee for this purpose, to make thee a minister and a witness both of these things which thou hast seen, and of those things in which I will appear unto thee;

18   To open their eyes, and to turn them from darkness to light, and from the power of Satan unto God, that they make receive forgiveness of sins, and inheritance among them which are sanctified by faith that is in me.

Romans 1:16-25

16   For I am not ashamed of the gospel of Christ: for it is the power of God unto salvation to every one that believeth; to the Jew first, and also to the Greek.
17   For therein is the righteousness of God revealed from faith to faith: as it is written, The just shall live by faith.
18   For the wrath of God is revealed from heaven against all ungodliness and unrighteousness of men, who hold the truth in unrighteousness;
19   Because that which may be known of God is manifest in them; for God hath showed it unto them.
20   For the invisible things of him from the creation of the world are clearly seen, being understood by the things that are made, even his eternal power and Godhead; so that they are without excuse:
21   Because that, when they knew God, they glorified him not as God, neither were thankful; but became vain in their imaginations, and their foolish heart was darkened.
22   Professing themselves to be wise, they became fools,
23   And changed the glory of the uncorruptible God into an image made like to corruptible man, and to birds, and fourfooted beasts, and creeping things.
24   Wherefore God also gave them up to uncleanness through the lusts of their own hearts, to dishonor their own bodies between themselves:
25   Who changed the truth of God into a lie, and worshipped and served the creature more than the Creator, who is blessed for ever. Amen.

Romans 6:1-4
1   What shall we say then? Shall we continue in sin, that grace may abound?
2   God forbid. How shall we, that are dead to sin, live any longer therein?
3   Know ye not, that so many of us as were baptized into Jesus Christ were baptized into his death?
4   Therefore we are buried with him by baptism into death: that like as Christ was raised up from the dead by the glory of the Father, even so we also should walk in newness of life.

Romans 6:15
15   What then? Shall we sin, because we are not under the law, but under grace? God forbid.

Romans 7:1-25
1   Know ye not, brethren, (for I speak to them that know the law,) how that the law hath dominion over a man as long as he liveth?
2   For the woman which hath an husband is bound by the law to her husband so long as he liveth; but if the husband be dead, she is loosed from the law of her husband.
3   So then if, while her husband liveth, she be married to another man, she shall be called an adulteress: but if her husband be dead, she is free from that law: so that she is no adulteress, though she be married to another man.
4   Wherefore, my brethren, ye also are dead to the law by the body of Christ; that he should be married to another, even to him who is raised from the dead, that we should bring forth fruit unto God.
5   For when we were in the flesh, the motions of sins, which were by the law, did work in our members to bring forth fruit unto death.

6   But now we are delivered from the law, that being dead wherein we were held; that we should serve in newness of spirit, and not in the oldness of the letter.

7   What shall we say then? Is the law sin? God forbid. Nay, I had not known sin, but by the law: for I had not known lust, except the law had said, Thou shalt not covet.

8   But sin, taking occasion by the commandment, wrought in me all manner of concupiscence. For without the law sin was dead.

9   For I was alive without the law once: but when the commandment came, sin revived, and I died.

10   And the commandment, which was ordained to life, I found to be undo death.

11   For sin, taking occasion by the commandment, deceived me, and by it slew me.

12   Wherefore the law is holy, and the commandment holy, and just, and good.

13   Was then that which is good made death unto me? God forbid. But sin, that is might appear sin, working death in me by that which is good; that sin by the commandment might become exceeding sinful.

14   For we know that the law is spiritual: but I am carnal, sold under sin.

15   For that which I do I allow not: for what I would, that do I not; but what I hate, that do I.

16   If then I do that which I would not, I consent unto the law that it is good.

17   Now then it is no more I that do it, but sin that dwelleth in me.

18   For I know that in me (that is, in my flesh,) dwelleth no good thing: for to will is present with me; but how to perform that which is good I find not.

19   For the good that I would I do not: but the evil which I would not, that I do.

20   Now if I do that I would not, it is no more I that do it, but sin that dwelleth in me.
21   I find then a law, that, when I would do good, evil is present with me.
22   For I delight in the law of God after the inward man:
23   But I see another law in my members, warring against the law of my mind, and bringing me into captivity to the law of sin which is in my members.
24   O wretched man that I am! Who shall deliver me from the body of this death?
25   I thank God through Jesus Christ our Lord. So then with the mind I myself serve the law of God; but with the flesh the law of sin.

Romans 7:2
2   For the woman which hath an husband is bound by the law to her husband so long as he liveth; but if the husband be dead, she is loosed from the law of her husband.

Romans 8:1-4
1   There is therefore now no condemnation to them which are in Christ Jesus, who walk not after the flesh, but after the Spirit.
2   For the law of the Spirit of life in Christ Jesus hath made me free from the law of sin and death.
3   For what the law could not do, in that it was weak through the flesh, God sending his own Son in the likeness of sinful flesh, and for sin, condemned sin in the flesh:
4   That the righteousness of the law might be fulfilled in us, who walk not after the flesh, but after the Spirit.

Romans 8:13-16
13   For if ye live after the flesh, ye shall die: but if ye through the Spirit do mortify the deeds of the body, ye shall live.

14   For as many as are led by the Spirit of God, they are the sons of God.
15   For ye have not received the spirit of bondage again to fear; but ye have received the Spirit of adoption, whereby we cry, Abba, Father.
16   The Spirit itself beareth witness with our spirit, that we are the children of God:

Romans 8:34
34   Who is he that condemneth? It is Christ that died, yea rather that is risen again, who is even at the right hand of God, who also maketh intercession for us.

Romans 8:35
35   Who shall separate us from the love of Christ? Shall tribulation, or distress, or persecution, or famine, or nakedness, or peril, or sword?

1 Corinthians 2:1-16
1   And I, brethren, when I came to you, came not with excellency of speech or of wisdom, declaring unto you the testimony of God.
2   For I determined not to know any thing among you, save Jesus Christ, and him crucified.
3   And I was with you in weakness, and in fear, and in much trembling.
4   And my speech and my preaching was not with enticing words of man's wisdom, but in demonstration of the Spirit and of power:
5   That your faith should not stand in the wisdom of men, but in the power of God.
6   Howbeit we speak wisdom among them that are perfect: yet not the wisdom of this world, nor of the princes of this world, that come to nought:

7   But we speak with the wisdom of God in a mystery, even the hidden wisdom, which God ordained before the world unto our glory.
8   Which none of the princes of this world knew: for had they known it, they would not have crucified the Lord of glory.
9   But as it is written, Eye hath not seen, nor ear heard, neither have entered into the heart of man, the things which God hath prepared for them that love him.
10   But God hath revealed them unto us by his Spirit: for the Spirit searcheth all things, yea, the deep things of God.
11   For what man knoweth the things of a man, save the spirit of man which is in him? Even so the things of God knoweth no man, but the Spirit of God.
12   Now we had received, not the spirit of the world, but the spirit which is God; that we might know the things that are freely given to us of God.
13   Which things also we speak, not in the words which man's wisdom teacheth, but which the Holy Ghost teacheth; comparing spiritual things with spiritual.
14   But the natural man receiveth not the things of the Spirit of God: for they are foolishness unto him: neither can he know them, because they are spiritually discerned.
15   But he that is spiritual judgeth all things, yet he himself is judged of no man.
16   For who hath known the mind of the Lord, that he may instruct him? But we have the mind of Christ.

1 Corinthians 8:3
3   But if any man love God, the same is known of him.

1 Corinthians 11:28
28   But let a man examine himself, and so let him eat of the bread, and drink of that cup.

1 Corinthians 13:13
13   And now abideth faith, hope, charity, these three; but the greatest of these is charity.

1 Corinthians 15:34
34   Awake to righteousness, and sin not; for some have not the knowledge of God; I speak this to your shame.

2 Corinthians 5:14
14   For the love of Christ constraineth us: because we thus judge, that if one died for all, then were all dead:

2 Corinthians 13:5
5   Examine yourselves, whether ye be in the faith; prove your own selves. Know ye not your own selves, how that Jesus Christ is in you, except ye be reprobates?

Galatians 2:20
20   I am crucified with Christ: nevertheless I live; not I, but Christ liveth in me: and the life which I now live in the flesh I live by the faith of the Son of God, who loved me, and gave himself for me.

Galatians 4:7-11
7   Wherefore thou art no more a servant, but a son; and if a son, then an heir of God through Christ.
8   Howbeit then, when ye knew not God, ye did service unto them which by nature are no gods.
9   But now, after that ye have known God, or rather are known of God, how turn ye again to the weak and beggarly elements, whereunto ye desire again to be in bondage?
10   Ye observe days, and months, and times, and years.
11   I am afraid of you, lest I have bestowed upon you labour in vain.

Galatians 5:1
1   Stand fast therefore in the liberty wherewith Christ hath make us free, and be not entangled again with the yoke of bondage.

Galatians 5:17
17   For the flesh lusteth against the Spirit, and the Spirit against the flesh: and these are contrary the one to the other: so that ye cannot do the things that ye would.

Galatians 6:1-10
1   Brethren, if a man be overtaken in a fault, ye which are spiritual, restore such an one in the spirit of meekness; considering thyself, lest thou also be tempted.
2   Bear ye one another's burdens, and so fulfil the law of Christ.
3   For if a man think himself to be something, when he is nothing, he deceiveth himself.
4   But let every man prove his own work, and then shall he have rejoicing in himself alone, and not in another.
5   For every man shall bear his own burden.
6   Let him that is taught in the word communicate unto him that teacheth in all good things.
7   Be not deceived; God is not mocked: for whatsoever a man soweth, that shall he also reap.
8   For he that soweth to his flesh shall of the flesh reap corruption; but he that soweth to the Spirit shall of the Spirit reap life everlasting.
9   And let us not be weary in well doing: for in due season we shall reap, if we faint not.
10   As we have therefore opportunity, let us do good unto all men, especially unto them who are of the household of faith.

Ephesians 1:22
22   And hath put all things under his feet, and gave him to be the head over all things to the church,

Ephesians 4:13
13   Till we all come in the unity of the faith, and of the knowledge of the Son of God, unto a perfect man, unto the measure of the stature of the fullness of Christ:

Ephesians 4:14-15
14   that we henceforth be no more children, tossed to and fro, and carried abut with every wind of doctrine, by the sleight of men, and cunning craftiness, whereby they lie in wait to deceive;
15   But speaking the truth in love, may grow up into him in all things, which is the head, even Christ:

Ephesians 4:25-32
25   Wherefore putting away lying, speak every man truth with his neighbor: for we are members one of another.
26   Be ye angry, and sin not: let not the sun go down upon your wrath:
27   Neither give place to the devil.
28   Let him that stole steal no more: but rather let him labour, working with his hands the thing which is good, that he may have to give to him that needeth.
29   Let no corrupt communication proceed out of your mouth, but that which is good to the use of edifying, that it may minister grace unto the hearers.
30   And grieve not the holy Spirit of God, whereby ye are sealed unto the day of redemption.
31   Let all bitterness, and wrath, and anger, and clamour, and evil speaking, be put away from you, with all malice:
32   And be ye kind one to another, tenderhearted, forgiving one another, even as God for Christ's sake hath forgiven you.

Ephesians 5:3-7

3   But fornication, and all uncleanness, or covetousness, let it not be once named among you, as becometh saints;

4   Neither filthiness, nor foolishtalking, nor jesting, which are not convenient: but rather giving of thanks.

5   For this ye know, that no whore-monger, nor unclean person, nor covetous man, who is an idolater, hath any interitance in the kingdom of Christ and of God.

6   Let no man deceive you with vain words: for because of these things cometh the wrath of God upon the children of disobedience.

7   Be not ye therefore partakers with them.

Ephesians 5:25-30

25   Husbands, love your wives, even as Christ also loved the church, and gave himself for it;

26   That he might sanctify and cleanse it with the washing of water by the word,

27   That he might present it to himself a glorious church, not having spot, or wrinkle, or any such thing; but that it should be holy and without blemish.

28   So ought men to love their wives as their own bodies. He that loveth his wife loveth himself.

29   For no man ever yet hated his own flesh; but nourisheth and clerisheth it, even as the Lord the church:

30   For we are members of his body, of his flesh, and of his bones.

Ephesians 5:31-33

31   For this cause shall a man leave his father and mother, and shall be joined unto his wife, and they two shall be one flesh,

32   This is the great mystery: but I speak concerning Christ and the church.

33   Nevertheless let every one of you in particular so love his wife even as himself; and the wife see that she reverence her husband.

Ephesians 6:10
10   Finally, my brethren, be strong in the Lord, and in the power of his might.

Ephesians 6:11
11   Put on the whole armor of God, that ye may be able to stand against the wiles of the devil.

Ephesians 6: 12-13
12   For we wrestle not against flesh and blood, but against principalities, against powers, against the rulers of the darkness of this world, against spiritual wickedness in high places.
13   Wherefore take unto you the whole armour of God, that ye may be able to withstand in the evil day, and having done all, to stand.

Ephesians 6:14-18
14   Stand therefore, having your loins girt about with truth, and having on the breastplate of righteousness;
15   And your feet shod with the preparation of the gospel of peace;
16   Above all, taking the shield of faith, wherewith ye shall be able to quench all the fiery darts of the wicked.
17   And take the helmet of salvation, and the sword of the Spirit, which is the word of God:
18   Praying always with all prayer and supplication in the Spirit, and watching thereunto with all perseverance and supplication for all saints;

Philippians 1:27
27   Only let your conversation be as it becometh the gospel of Christ: that whether I come and see you, or else be absent, I may hear of your affairs, that ye stand fast in one spirit, with one mine striving together for the faith of the gospel.

Philippians 2:5-8
5   Let this mind be in you, which was also in Christ Jesus:
6   Who, being in the form of God, thought it not robbery to be equal with God:
7   But made himself of no reputation, and took upon him the form of a servant, and was made in the likeness of men:
8   And being found in fashion as a man, he humbled himself, and became obedient unto death, even the death of the cross.

Colossians 1:20
20   And, having made peace through the blood of his cross, by him to reconcile all things unto himself; by him, I say, whether they be things in earth, or things in heaven.

Colossians 3:10
10   And have put on the new man, which is renewed in knowledge after the image of him that created him:

Colossians 4:5
5   Walk in wisdom toward them that are without, redeeming the time.

2 Timothy 2:15
15   Study to show thyself approved unto God, a workman that needeth not to be ashamed, rightly dividing the word of truth.

2 Timothy 3:16-17

16   All scripture is given by inspiration of God, and is profitable for doctrine, for reproof, for correction, for instruction in righteousness:

17   That the man of God may be perfect, thoroughly furnished unto all good works.

2 Timothy 4:1-5

1   I charge thee therefore before God, and the Lord Jesus Christ, who shall judge the quick and the dead at his appearing and his kingdom;

2   Preach the word; be instant in season, out of season; reprove, rebuke, exhort with all longsuffering and doctrine.

3   For the time will come when they will not endure sound doctrine; but after their own lusts shall they heap to themselves teachers, having itching ears;

4   And they shall turn away their ears from the truth, and shall be turned unto fables.

5   But watch thou in all things, endure afflictions, do the work of an evangelist, make full proof of thy ministry.

Titus 2:13

13   Looking for that blessed hope, and the glorious appearing of the great God and our Saviour Jesus Christ;

Philemon 1:17-19

17   If thou count me therefore a partner, receive him as myself.

18   If he hath wronged thee, or oweth thee ought, put that on mine account;

19   I Paul have written it with mine own hand. I will repay it: albeit I do not say to thee how thou owest unto me even tine own self besides.

Philemon 1:20-21
20   Yea, brother, let me have joy of thee in the Lord: refresh my bowels in the Lord.
21   Having confidence in thy obedience I wrote unto thee, knowing that thou will do more than I say.

Hebrews 11:25
25   Choosing rather to suffer affliction with the people of God, than to enjoy the pleasures of sin for a season;

Hebrews 12:2
2   Looking unto Jesus the author and finisher of our faith; who for the joy that was set before him endured the cross, despising the shame, and is set down at the right hand of the throne of God.

Hebrews 12:5-10
5   And ye have forgotten the exhortation which speaketh unto you as unto children, My son, despise not thou the chastening of the Lord, nor faint when thou art rebuked of him:
6   For whom the Lord loveth he chasteneth, and scourgeth every son whom he receiveth.
7   If ye endure chastening, God dealeth with you as with sons; for what son is he whom the father chasteneth not?
8   But if ye be without chastisement, whereof all are partakers, then are ye bastards, and not sons.
9   Furthermore we have had fathers of our flesh which corrected us, and we have them reverence: shall we not much rather be in subjection unto the Father of spirits, and live?
10   For they verily for a few days chastened us after their own pleasure; but he for our profit, that we might be partakers of his holiness.

Hebrews 13:4
4 Marriage is honourable in all, and the bed undefiled: but whoremongers and adulterers God will judge.

Hebrew 13:7
7 Remember them which have the rule over you, who have spoken unto you the word of God: whose faith follow, considering the end of their conversation.

Hebrews 13:8
8 Jesus Christ the same yesterday, and to day, and for ever.

1 Peter 1:15-16
15 But as he which hath called you is holy, so be ye holy in all manner of conversation;
16 Because it is written, Be ye holy; for I am holy.

1 Peter 2:9
9 But ye are a chosen generation, a royal priesthood, an holy nation, a peculiar people; that ye should show forth the praises of him who hath called you out of darkness into his marvelous light:

1 Peter 3:22
22 Who is gone into heaven, and is on the right hand of God; angels and authorities and powers being made subject unto him.

2 Peter 2:4
4 For if God spared not the angels that sinned, but cast them down to hell, and delivered them into chains of darkness, to be reserved unto judgment;

2 Peter 2:14,18

14   Having eyes full of adultery, and that cannot cease from sin; beguiling unstable souls: an heart they have exercised with covetous practices; cursed children:

18   For when they speak great swelling words of vanity, they allure through the lusts of the flesh, through much wantonness, those that were clean escaped from them who live in error.

1 John 2:1-6

1   My little children, these things write I unto you, that ye sin not. And if any man sin, we have an advocate with the Father, Jesus Christ the righteous:

2   And he is the propitiation for our sins: and not for ours only, but also for the sins of the whole world.

3   And hereby we do know that we know him, and we keep his commandments.

4   He that saith, I know him, and keepeth not his commandments, is a liar, and the truth is not in him.

5   But whoso keepeth his word, in him verily is the love of God perfected: hereby know we that we are in him.

6   He that saith he abideth in him ought himself also so to walk, even as he walked.

1 John 3:1-10

1   Behold, what manner of love the Father hath bestowed upon us, that we should be called the sons of God: therefore the world knoweth us not, because it knew him not.

2   Beloved, now are we the sons of God, and it doth not yet appear what we shall be: but what know that, when he shall appear, we shall be like him; for we shall see him as he is.

3   And every man that hath this hope in him purifieth himself, even as he is pure.

4   Whosoever committeth sin transgresseth also the law: for sin is the transgression of the law.

5   And ye know that he was manifested to take away our sins; and in him is no sin.
6   Whosoever abideth in him sineth not: whosoever sinneth hath not seen him, neither known him.
7   Little children, let no man deceive you: he that doeth righteousness is righteous, even as he is righteous.
8   He that committeth sin is of the devil; for the devil sinneth from the beginning. For this purpose the Son of God was manifested, that he might destroy the works of the devil.
9   Whosoever is born of God doth not commit sin; for his seed remaineth in him: and he cannot sin, because he is born of God.
10   In this the children of God are manifest, and the children of the devil: whosoever doeth not righteousness is not of God, neither he that loveth not his brother.

1 John 3:16
16   Hereby perceive we the love of God, because he laid down his life for us: and we ought to lay down our lives for the brethren.

1 John 4:1-6
1   Beloved, believe not every spirit, but try the spirits whether they are of God: because many false prophets are gone out into the world.
2   Hereby know ye the Spirit of God: Every spirit that confesseth that Jesus Christ is come in the flesh is of God:
3   And every spirit that confesseth not that Jesus Christ is come in the flesh is not of God: and this is that spirit of antichrist, whereof ye have heard that it should come; and even now already is it in the world.
4   Ye are of God, little children, and have overcome them: because greater is he that is in you, than he that is in the world.
5   They are of the world: therefore speak they of the world, and the world heareth them.

6   We are of God: he that knowth God heareth us; he that is not of God heareth not us. Hereby know we the spirit of truth, and the spirit of error.

1 John 4:8
8   He that loveth not knoweth not God; for God is love.

James 1:17
17   Every good gift and every perfect gift is from above, and cometh down from the Father of lights, with whom is no variableness, neither shadow of turning.

James 1:22
22   But be ye doers of the word, and not hearers only, deceiving your own selves.
23   For if any be a hearer of the word, and not a doer, he is like unto a man beholding his natural face in a glass:
24   For he beholdeth himself, and goeth his way, and straightway forgeteth what manner of man he was.

James 4:7
7   Submit yourselves therefore to God. Resist the devil, and he will flee from you.

Revelation 3:14-22
14   And unto the angel of the church of the Laodiceans write; These things saith the Amen, the faithful and true witness, the beginning of the creation of God;
15   I know thy works, that thou art neither cold nor hot: I would thou wert cold or hot.
16   So then because thou art luke-warm, and neither cold nor hot, I will spue thee out of my mouth.

17   Because thou sayest, I am rich, and increased with goods, and have need of nothing; and knowest not that thou art wretched, and miserable, and poor, and blind, and naked:
18   I counsel thee to buy of me gold tried in the fire, that thou mayest be rich; and white raiment, that thou mayest be clothed, and that the shame of thy nakedness do not appear; and anoint thine eyes with eyesalve, that thou mayest see.
19   As many as I love, I rebuke and chasten: be zealous therefore, and repent.
20   Behold, I stand at the door, and knock: if any man hear my voice, and open the door, I will come in to him, and will sup with him, and he with me.
21   To him that overcometh will I grant to sit with me in my throne, even as I also overcame, and am set down with my Father in his throne.
22   He that hath an ear, let him hear what the Spirit saith unto the churches.

Revelation 3:15
15   I know thy words, that thou art neither cold nor hot: I would thou wert cold or hot.

Revelation 3:20
20   Behold, I stand at the door, and knock: if any man hear my voice, open the door, I will come in to him, and will sup with him, and he with me.

Revelation 3:21-22
21   To him that overcometh will I grant to sit with me in my throne, even as I also overcame, and am set down with my Father in his throne.
22   He that hath an ear, let him hear what the Spirit saith unto the churches.

Revelation 19:6
6   And I heard as it were the voice of a great multitude, and as the voice of many waters, and as the voice of mighty thunderings, saying Alleluia: for the Lord God omnipotent reigneth.

Revelation 21:5
5   And he that sat upon he throne said, Behold, I make all things new. And he said unto me, Write, for these words are true and faithful.

Revelation 22:6
6   And he said unto me, These sayings are faithful and true: and the Lord God of the holy prophets sent his angel to show unto his servants the things which must shortly be done.

Revelation 22:19
19   And if any man shall take away from the words of the book of this prophecy, God shall take away his part out of the book of life, and out of the holy city, and form the things which are written in this book.

About Evangelist Beverly Yokley

Beverly Burros Yokley was born in Akron, Ohio on March 2, 1947 to the late Tom and Sarah (Woods) Burros. She was united in marriage to Elder Charles S. Yokley on January 5, 1974 – August 16, 2017 (deceased); and to this union four children were born: Tabitha Dean (P. Jeremiah) Satterfield, Dr. Delight Bena Yokley, PhD., David Israel (Laura) Newberry-Yokley and Charles Stanley (Shauntina) Yokley, II.

She lived and worked in Akron, Springfield and Cleveland, OH, Columbia, TN and now resides in Dickson, TN.

She attended:
- Cedarville Baptist College; September 11, 1978 – March 16, 1979
- Moody Bible Institute; January – May 1994
- Ashland Theological Seminary; September 1997 – May 1998
- Wright State University; graduate with BS in Business Administration in June 1989

Evangelist Beverly Yokley has been a member of The Original Church of God – Sanctified Church since 1968 and an Ordained Minister since 1974. Evangelist Yokley has over 40 years of services.

Her life verse is Galatians 2:20 "I am crucified with Christ: nevertheless I live; yet not I, but Christ liveth in me: and the life which I now live in the flesh I live by the faith of the Son of God, who loved me, and gave himself for me."

The **<u>Lights Out Midnight</u>** sermon was given to her by the Lord while in the hospital after being delivered from Transverse Myelitis (a disorder caused by inflammation of the spinal cord). Other sermons were included as the Lord gave them.

About Laura Newberry-Yokley

Laura Newberry-Yokley has always been a spiritual sojourner and writer all of her life. She was born in Boulder, Colorado in 1980. Laura earned a Master of Arts in Women's Studies in Religion from Claremont Graduate University in Claremont, California.

Immediately following graduating from The College of Wooster, she lived in India at the base of the Himalayan Mountains. After graduating from graduate school, Laura traveled again in India in 2005 and 2006.

Upon returning to the United States, Laura moved to Columbus, Ohio, where she worked as a health policy strategist for eight years. She learned about what it means to be a business woman, which includes learning a very different genre of writing: business jargon, health policy strategy, white papers, and legislative language. She also partnered with African American and Hispanic groups, helping harness language and culture to move business forward and close health disparity gaps in minority communities. Her work has been recognized by the Gospel Heritage Foundation and the National Organization of Black Elected Legislative Women (NOBEL).

Since 2015, Laura has worked for a local United Way in rural Ohio in marketing and engagement. She is a Bridges Out of Poverty trainer and has trained over one thousand participants (lawyers, teachers, social workers, and community members) on how to understand local poverty and how to eradicate it.

Her goal has always been to give voice to the voiceless, access to the shut out, and visibility to those who need a spotlight.

Laura's role in the **Lights Out at Midnight** project has been to organize a platform for Evangelist Yokley to share her sermons with a larger community of pastors and practitioners. In 2014, Laura began organizing and typing Evangelist Yokley's sermon notes and compiling them into five unique sections.

Laura attended:
- BA, Spanish & Classical Studies, The College of Wooster, Ohio (2003)
- MA, Women's Studies in Religion, Claremont Graduate University, California (2006)

Laura is the President and CEO of Sonrisa Products, a holistic leadership company.

About the Publisher

Sonrisa Products is a holistic leadership company that provides authentic leadership solutions to businesses, governments, educational institutions, nonprofit organizations, and communities. Through language acquisition and cultural innovation, as well as self-exploration, we assist you in opening to new opportunities to become a savvier you.

Sonrisa Products creates tools and techniques geared toward self-awareness, opening, expanding, and grounding. The unique product lines assist those who desire a fresh take on leadership.
Visit **www.sonrisaproducts.com** for more information.

Notes:

Notes:

Notes:

Notes:

www.ingramcontent.com/pod-product-compliance
Lightning Source LLC
LaVergne TN
LVHW051545070426
835507LV00021B/2418